Realities of Life
A Book of Poetry ... and more

Wanda Muir-Oliver

Realities Of Life™
~~WAMO~~ Publishing
P.O. Box 1596
Ellicott City, MD 21041

Realities of Life

A Book of Poetry ... and more
By Wanda Muir-Oliver

Published by WAMO Publishing
P.O. Box 1596, Ellicott City, MD 21041

All rights reserved. No part of this book may be reproduced or transmitted in any form or by any means, electronic or mechanical, including photocopying, recording, or by any information storage or retrieval system without the prior written permission from the author, except for the inclusion of brief quotations in a review.

First Printing - December 2005
Copyright 2005 by Wanda Muir-Oliver
Graphics: Kamau Francis Sennaar for Inspire Art Company
Photo Credits: Front Cover - Steve Cuffie
Photo Credits: Author's Biography Page - Betty Stratford
Twin Towers Illustration: Nedra Lowery (Age 16)
Printed by BCP Digital
Printed in the United States of America

1. Poetry
2. Fiction
3. Self Improvement

ISBN Number: 0-9773336-0-4
Library of Congress Catalog Card Number: 5555-1212-7
Soft Cover
$19.00

Some proceeds from this book will go to the American Diabetes Association (Stroke Division), the National Breast Cancer Foundation, Katrina (DST) and National Council of Negro Women Youth Programs.

Book Dedication

This book is dedicated to my father and mother whom I love greatly, and for instilling in me a spirit of peace. I am humble and grateful that you taught me to be a giver to others early in my life - something that I am still carrying out today.

I am continuously being blessed because of the early instruction and tools given to me by you. I am blessed.

Thank you. I love you.

Realities of Life

FOREWORD ix
A Foreword by Dr. Dorothy I. Height

ACKNOWLEDGMENTS x

CHAPTER 1
Spirituality

Realities Of Life	2
Poetry	5
Dream	7
A Dream	8
A Feeling of Ease	9
A Love For Snow	10
A Wake Up From You	11
Breaking Free	12
Christmas Time	13
Fashion Flair	14
Girlfriends	15
God's Gift	17
God Opened My Eyes	18
Gone A Little While	20
Healing	21
It Is Not Just My Agenda	22
I Want To	23
Just Pray	26
Realities Of Life: Personal Quotes	27
Seasons of Change	28

Table of Contents

Thanksgiving	29
The Change	30
Transformed By God	31
Unsinned	32
You Are The Source of My Strength	33
You Tried To Steal My Joy	34
You Were Always There For Me	35

CHAPTER 2
Love

Love Is	37
To Love Someone	38
A Meeting A Thrill	39
You Danced With Me	40
Wonderful Thoughts of You	41
When I Am With You	42
A Stare of Surprise	43
My Prince Charming	44
You Are Unreal	45
Wedding Day	46
A Kiss of a Different Kind	47
Feeling You	48
Unconditionally Love	50
You	51
Your Opened and Closed Spirit	52
Runaway Love	53
I Enjoyed Your Company	55
An Affair	57

Realities of Life

A Relationship Gone Bad	59
Why You Want To Act Like That	60
Anger	63
My Tears	64
A Heart Once Captured	65
You're Not The Perfect One	66
I Want Sunshine Too	67
Love	68
You Were There	69
No Longer A Friend	70
You Taught Me Lessons The Hard Way	72
This Weight Is A Problem	74
Mental Equation	75
Music	76
What Makes Me Happy	77
Inspire	78
Loving Self	79

CHAPTER 3
Honor and Cherish

Mother	81
Father	82
Grandmothers	83
Sisters	84
Elders We Thank You	85
A Death Of A Loved One	86
Aunt	87
Children Of Innocence	88

Table of Contents

Delivery	89
Friendship Is A Gift	90
Give To Oneself	91
Mentor	92
Our Wedding Day	93
Rememberance	94
Special One	95
Teacher	96
Thank You Mary McLeod Bethune	97
When I Think About You	99

CHAPTER 4
Society

911	102
A Bus Ride Home	103
A Changing World	105
A Day Erased	107
A Job	109
A Rapid Changing World	110
Choices	112
Crime	113
Driving	114
Education Is A Tool	115
In the Congo	116
Leadership	117
Leadership Qualities	119
Money	120

Realities of Life

The New Generation	122
What Is Leadership?	125
Katrina	128

CHAPTER 5
Conversations: Short Stories

Dead But Still Living	131
Kitchen Spy	135
Reunited Again	139
The Family Gatherings Growing Up	145
Yesterday's Beginnngs	157

Author's Biography   165

Foreword

Here is a collection that quite properly fulfills the essence of its title - "***Realities of Life***." Using different poetic styles and some essays, the author gives glimpses of experiences to which we find it easy to relate. In the brief essays of real people doing real things, we gain insight into remarkable personalities.

I found very special meaning in reading about Mary McLeod Bethune who was so often described as if she were an institution or an organization. The author, with this collection, projects her as the person I knew and worked with day by day. Her intellect, her organizational skills and deeply rooted spirituality come through and helps to light the way for others. I did not know the others whose lives are described, but reading about them made me feel at home with them. I felt that they were a part of my own reality.

By calling this collection "***Realities of Life***," the author reminds us of the blessings of life which everyday open up to us all that is real, absolute and unchangeable. We have to be grateful for this collection which, as we enjoy it, will stimulate us to learn to appreciate and to face reality.

Dr. Dorothy I. Height
Chair/President Emerita
National Council of Negro Women, Inc.
May 25, 2005

Realities of Life

I would like to thank my mentor Dr. Dorothy I. Height who agreed to write the foreword for this book and took time out of her busy schedule to do so. I am grateful.

There are too many good words to write down that describe how awesome you are as an individual. Your talks with me and sharing your wisdom have enriched me greatly and will be a part of my spirit as long as I shall live. "I am blessed to have met you, a strong vibrant woman full of purpose."

You have pushed me to do my best leading by example with your exceptional leadership skills and services caring for others.

I respect you for your honesty, integrity and sincerity. Your foreword to my book, "***Realities of Life***" has added substance and a dimension that coincides with professionalism at its best. Thank you for your gift and helping me with my journey. I love you.

Wanda Muir-Oliver
June 2005

Acknowledgements

When writing this book, there were many challenges in getting this project done. It seemed to be a set back every time that we thought we were moving forward or planning to have the book done by a certain date or a certain time. There were illnesses, hospital stays, and schedule delays.

But through the realization of all of the occurrences of things there is a time and a season for everything, we are not in control of things and it has to be within God's timing when we finalize things.

I am blessed with a multitude of love ones within my life. There are so many people who have helped me with my journey along the way...

Thank you Bishop elect Dr. Walter Scott Thomas and Sister Thomas for your valuable instruction of the word. It has been a blessing to my soul and motivation.

I would like to thank my daughter Ericka L. Oliver (Spelmanite) who took time out of her hectic work schedule to be my editor-in-chief for this book and my future son-in-law, Craig Brooks for being supportive of her and me during this time. Ericka, you are a joy too. "I love you both." I also express my deep love for my son Brian Oliver.

I would like to thank my biological sisters Lauren and Merle for their love, encouragement and support that

Realities of Life

has always been a given. I can count on you no matter what. We have enjoyed reading over my poems, talking about them and laughing at many of them. Your suggestions and criticism I value straight from the heart.

    I would like to thank my niece Nedra Lowery (age 16) for drawing the Twin Towers to serve as the background for my poem "911". Nedra, you did a good job with no ruler, no tools, except pencil and paper. You truly have a gift, and my hope is that you continue to use it. I am looking forward to receiving your graphic design for my upcoming novel.

    I would like to thank my Aunt Ernie and Uncle Grice. When my mother was in the hospital for quite some time, you took care of me along with my dad. You dressed me and combed my hair and made sure I went to school looking good. You always prompted me being the best that I could be through doing my work in school and getting my education. Although you often entertained celebrities and we were in their presence, you always kept everything real and kept us focused. Your constant encouragement has helped me to become successful today.

    Brenda Coleman Lipscomb (cos) thank you for all of your support and your reading of my works. Your kind words and support have been a blessing to me.

Acknowledgements

Phyllis Lee and Sandra Jackson, my adopted sisters - thanks for always listening to my poetry growing up and listening to it today. You have always been supportive of me. Thanks!

Thank you, Helen Dale and Dr. Dabeth S. Manns for helping me on such short notice with the editing of the book. How kind of you... I am appreciative of all that you do. The time and effort that you have taken out of your time to help me is greatly appreciated. Your suggestions were enlightening in how to improve my writing. Your expertise in this area has been exceptional in helping to bring things to closure for this project. Thanks for your inspiration and guidance. You have truly been a blessing to me.

I like to thank my mentor Dr. Thelma T. Daley for her wisdom, leadership and for giving of herself to expose me to positive and productive things. I have so much respect for you. Your expertise in speaking has permeated my realm of thinking and has altered my thoughts about what to say before I speak. Your motivation has been a blessing, stressing the importance for me to keep moving in the right direction and to never let anything get in my way of accomplishing what I want or set out to do. You taught me not to run when things become difficult, to stay still and work towards change. You have nurtured

Realities of Life

---

my leadership by example. You always have a willingness to be a giver. Also, I like to thank you for being one of my trusted rough draft readers.

    Althea Alston Wilson (Peachie) we have been best friends since middle school, and although we live distances apart from one another, it does not make a difference. We always seem to be able to pick up where ever we left off with one another. Our chemistry is such a good mix. Your support, honesty and positivity has always been a given. Thank you for reading over some of my rough drafts.

    I like to thank my line sister Lisa Lee-Packer who has always been supportive of whatever it is that I plunge into, and who has taken a great deal of time to read over my rough drafts. We are comfortable with one another no matter what the mood. Of course, I knew that you would give constructive criticism and always there to be supportive of me when I need you too.

    Joanne Christopher Hicks thank you for all of your support at Coppin State University. All of your help has been valuable to me.

    I would like to thank my graphics producer Kamau Sennaar who worked diligently on this project and treated it as if it was his own project. Kamau did everything that he could do to help make this project a

Acknowledgements

success. I would also like to thank Lisa Mitchell Sennaar (Kamau's wife) for your dialog with me and for supporting Kamau's long hours when working on this project and for your encouragement to me as well.

Thank you Pat Jessamy for taking the time out of your busy schedule and finding the time to read my materials while on a plane off to work. Your laughter with some of the poems let me know that the art of poetry was working. Your encouragement and support has been appreciative.

Thank you Valerie Frailing and Michele Emery for listening to my readings for hours at a time, as I read my poetry to you and having your say about it. Thank you for your support and encouragement.

Teressa Boston, thank you for helping me whenever there was a need. I can always count on you. Thank you for reading my rough drafts.

Angela Ray, thank you for reading my works and being supportive of my work, staying in touch and giving much encouragement. I enjoyed performing with you on stage in Las Vegas, Nevada. I wish you continued success in your television and movie performances.

Thank you, Diana Wharton Sennaar (an original member of "Sweet Honey In The Rock") and her husband

Realities of Life

A.D. Sennaar for your consulting and taking time out to give me valuable information in the area of the arts and promoting. I wish you continued success with Tauhid Institute in Baltimore, MD.

A thanks to Mugsey Bogues (NBA) for giving me the opportunity to direct your basketball extended camp and for giving me the opportunity to deliver poetry to the children.

Thank you cousin Louis Diggs (founder of the Black Writers' Guild of Maryland, Inc.) and Shirley Diggs for supporting me and giving much praise on my accomplishment of writing and finishing this book. The Black Writers' Guild has given me so much education and exposure to other renowned artists as well as workshops that covered so many different areas of the arts. Both of you have inspired me to keep moving on to higher ground.

Dr. E.A. Betty Edmonds, you have truly been an inspiration with your encouragement and insight as a professor in the educational field which has helped to propel my thinking to a different level.

Verna Day-Jones (Ms. Senior Maryland 2004-2005) I have enjoyed performing with you and appreciate you sharing your wisdom of the pros and cons when competing within the industry. Your insight has given me much throughout and has shown me how to carry out

Acknowledgements

things. You are always giving, and giving everything at your best. That's why you are Ms. Senior Maryland.

I would like to thank Dr. Lavon Bracey, a dear friend to our family, for your encouragement when we had our discussion twenty years ago (sitting around the kitchen table) about me writing a book, and the promise that I kept to myself. It is finally coming to fruition.

I'd like to thank you Christine Toney and Lola Early for your assistance when ever it was needed. Your help has been appreciated.

I'd like to thank Betty Stratford for your support and your professional picture shoots of me and Dr. Dorothy I. Height. By the way, the pictures are beautiful!

Kitty Chaney, thank you for introducing me to a few well known authors who were presenting their works and giving me the opportunity to introduce my book and dialog with them.

Michelle Holden - thank you for your support and assistance.

Cheryl Cooper , thank you for your kind words, inspiration and listening to my readings.

Sara Fan, thank you for designing a beautiful website displaying my book with some of my writings. Much gratitude.

Realities of Life

Minnie Carter, thank you for putting my picture along with a poem in your "Hope, Faith and Patriotism" book. It was so thoughtful and kind of you to include me. Also thank you for listening to my poetry at the Guild. I have also enjoyed performing with you on stage.

Thank you, Yvonne Jones (Tallwood High School, Virginia Beach, VA) for proofreading my poetry, research papers and editing other works of mine while I was in college. As an English teacher, you gave suggestions on how to improve upon my writing. As a result, you saw growth and great improvement in my writings. Thanks for your support and encouragement.

To Diane Lewis and Pam Englemen (Owen Brown Middle School, Columbia, MD - 2000), I am grateful for the two of you. You were my support mechanism when I was working full time and attending school. You proofread some of my research papers and offered your suggestions. Also, some of my poetry, read by you and your students, appears in this book.

Thank you Phyllis McCants (Professor, Tidewater Community College, Virginia Beach, VA.) for reviewing and helping me with improving my work when I was college student enrolled in two of your classes. Some of the work I wrote in Virginia is included in this book. Thank you for your encouragement and support. Much love. You are wonderful!

Acknowledgements

Olivia Dabney and Bernard Morgan, you all were the best principals around when you were in Virginia Beach, VA. Sometimes it takes some time to realize what an impact someone has made on you when you go somewhere to work. Your leadership skills were the best in the business. Thanks for showing me the ropes.

Shirley Barbara, thanks for always being supportive of me and listening and reading my poetry while I was a student and giving of yourself.

Sonya Archer and Nicollette Hunter, thank you for your support and assistance.

Thanks to Reg Hahn for your help and assistance in developing such beautiful colorful cards for me with my book cover shown. Your help has been appreciated.

Thanks to all of my immediate aunts and uncles: Aunt Dot, Uncle Sesera, Aunt Helen, Uncle Lindsey, Uncle Chink, Aunt Phyliss, Uncle Arthur, Aunt Margie, Uncle Adolph, Aunt Doris, Uncle Clint, Aunt Merle, Uncle Tim, Aunt Ruth, Uncle Kenneth and all of my cousins. All of you have always been supportive in whatever I attempted to do.

Thank you everyone who sits on the executive board with me within the Black Writers' Guild of Maryland, Inc. Your support and sharing of works together has been

Realities of Life

a blessing to us all - Louis Diggs, Dr. Evangeline Wheeler, Minnie Carter, Brenda Degraffiend, Jim Wright and Emma Graves.

Rita Cooper, Gwen Lindsey, Kathy McLaughlin, Ruthie Hall, Dr. Jackie Williams, Joanne Otis, Stephanie Lee, Louisiana Jefferson, Dr. Margaret Turner, Yvonne Smith and Linda Carter - always giving the proper training in order to matriculate into other areas. Thank you for all of your leadership motivation and support.

I would like to thank the organizations ZE - Delta Sigma Theta (DST) - Renaissance (29) 2000, Coppin State University, we are blessed! Thanks for giving of oneself.

Thank you Beverly Boston, Delta Sigma Theta, Inc. (BAC).

I also would like to thank the organizations who has supported me: **Delta Sigma Theta, Inc. -** the love that you have shown and the sisterhood given to me has been so beautiful. Thank you sorors for supporting me. "I love all of you." Delta has truly given me a thirst for knowledge and has enhanced my leadership capabilities to another level. Thank you Delta for helping me to live up to my highest potential.

Acknowledgements

A thank you to other organizations for your support: National Council of Negro Women Inc. (Washington D.C.), National Congress of Black Women, Howard County Education Association (Joe Stubb and staff), Maryland State Teachers Association, Black Writers' Guild of Maryland, Inc. (Baltimore, MD), Howard County Park and Recreation (Columbia, MD), Columbia Association (Columbia, MD), Virginia Business and Professional Women Inc. (Virginia Beach, VA), Virginia Beach Education Association (Virginia Beach, VA), Delta T Group (Columbia, MD - Eric and Collette), Women of Responsive Government (Maryland), Healing Hands Wellness Center, Inc. (Atlanta, GA), Commission for Women (Columbia, MD), Affinity Groups, LLC (Atlanta, GA), The Links (Maryland), Howard County Public Schools (Ellicott City, MD), Mid Towne Medical (Baltimore, MD), National Musuem of Women In The Arts (Washington, DC), Phi Theta Kappa members, Coppin State University (Baltimore, MD) Departments of Special Education, Psychology and Social Work, Morgan State University (Baltimore, MD), 100 Black Women (Baltimore, MD), 100 Black Men (Baltimore, MD), Continentals (Baltimore, MD), Zeta Phi Beta Inc., Alpha Kappa Alpha, Inc., Sigma Gamma Rio, Inc., Omega Psi Phi, Inc., Iota Kappa Alpha Psi, Inc., Muir Little Scholars, Radio KTYM-1460 AM (Donny Anderson - CA), 92Q, 95.9, 88.9 (Sandi Mallory/Gary "Primetime" Ellerbe), Heaven 600 AM (Lee Michaels),

Realities of Life

WOLB 1010 AM (Larry Young), 104.3 FM - MD (Randy Dennis), WHUR - Washigton, D.C. (Tricina Gray), Woodbourne Center (Baltimore, MD), Howard County Education Association, Virginia Beach Education Association, Columbia, MD, Personality Hair, (Ellicott City, MD), Tauhid Institute, Staples (Shannon Holden - Ellicott City, MD), Rose Breast Cancer Society (Los Angeles, California), Black Issues (NY), People On The Move (Baltimore County, MD), Women Power (Baltimore, MD), NAACP, Urban League, Masons Lodge (Delaware), Germantown Hospital (Philadelphia, PA), Tidewater Community College, Virginia Beach, VA, The Philadelphia Inquirer, The Ledger (Virginia), The Washington Times (Washington, D.C.), The Sun Newspaper, The Baltimore Times, The Howard County Times, The Ellicott City Times, Enoch Pratt Free Public Library, Howary County Public Library, Black Classic Press (Baltimore, MD), Dr. Lavon Bracey, Ursula Battle, Dr. Battle (President, Coppin University), Cathy Bell (Radio One), Cadelia Birdsong (Notary), Dr. Eloise Bridges, Beverly Boston, the Afro American Newspaper (Baltimore, MD), Althoton High School, Urban League.

I would like to thank others who read through my brochure and viewed a couple of sneak peaks of poems that would be applied to my book: Dr. Joyce Agunbiade, Kathy Alexander, Cecil Alleyne, Althea Alston-Wilson, Anthony Anderson, Curt Anderson, Stanice Anderson,

Acknowledgements

Francina Bean-Waters, Dr. Fahiem Boyd, Joanne Boyd, Kendall Boyd, Zach Boyd, Bryan Brooks, Dr. Karen Brown, Dr. Jackie Brown, Timmy Brown, Linda Joy Burke, Dr. Charla Butler, Sheila Butler, Dr. Julius Chapman, Kevin Carr, Stephanie Carr, Kahliah Carter, Minnie Carter, Robert Carter, Kitty Chaney, Brenda Conley, Marvin "Doc" Cheatham, Rita Cooper, Anne West-Clark, Johnny Clinton, Martina Clinton, Ryan Coleman, Estelle Collins, Elijah Cummings, Olivia Dabney, Grady Dale, Ann Delacy, Keshia Denson, Dr. Barbara Dandridge, Sheila Dixon, Elizabeth, Marietta English, Yvette Finney, Diana Ford, Elenora Forward, Annie Foster, Sam Foster, Jacqueline Frierson, Patricia Gaines, Cheryl Gail, Karla Garisson, Harriett Gaskins, George George, Pauline George, Cassandra Goldberg, Brian Goldberg, Sara Gray, Vernon Gray, Laura Gouch, Louise C. Green III, Ernistine Grice, The Hamms, Yvonne Harrison, Bill Harvey, Antonio Hayes, Debra Hayes, Dr. Donald Hayes, Dr. Carla Hayden, Barbara Hill, Dr. Vonda Smith-Hill, Joanne Christopher Hicks, Francine Holden, Helen Holden, Linwood Holden, Margret Holden, Michelle Holden, Sadie Howell, Yvonne Howell, Chante Hunter, Jackie Hunter, Jean Hyche-Jackson, Cassandra Jackson, Jerome Jefferson, Edith Jenkins, Herbert Jenkins, Coach "Butch" Johnson, Barbara Johnson, Aubrey Jones, Kaliah Jones, Robbie Jones, Verna Day-Jones, Linda Kimbrough, Lisa Kimbrough, Phyllis Veris Lee, Diane Lewis, Beverly Lloyd, Barbara Love, Mary Matlock, Tee

Realities of Life

Matlock, Anthony McCarthy, Cheryl McCloud, Selima Marriott, Kweisi Mfume, Serena Mills, Clarence Mitchell III, Keiffer Mitchell Jr., Steve Mitchell, Merritine Moore, Dr. Evordon Morton, Adolph Muir, Doris Muir, Laurie Muir, Lauren Muir, lil Merle Muir, Margo Muir, Merle Muir, Phyllis Muir, Qlinton Muir, Thomas Muir, Tanya Muir, Warren Muir, Warren Muir Jr., Bishop Vashti McKenzie, Frankie Lou Murphy, Louise Murphy, Dr. Rolunda Murray, Nana, Alice Oliver, Brian Oliver, Kevin Oliver, Michelle Oliver, Warren Oliver, Cheryl Pasteur, Mammie Perkins, Margret Proctor, Catherine Pugh, Charles Prather, Jackie Prather, Toby Pulley, Dave Rakes, Angela Ray, Dr. Barbara Reynolds, Jackie Richerson, Betty Robinson, Steve Shaffer, Gary Scott, Wanda Scott, Tavis Smiley, Audrey Smith, Dr. Ian Smith, Nijah Smith, Ronnie Smith, Yvonne Smith, Candi Strickland, Toney Strickland, Shirley Stokes, Vera Tanksley, Dr. Brenda Willis Taylor, Debra Taylor, Dr. George Taylor, Joy Thomas, Kathleen Kennedy Townsend, Dr. Margaret Turner, Connie Unseld, Wes Unseld, Senator John Warner, Samuel Washington, Pauline Watson, Dr. Evangeline Wheeler, Cheryl White, Darlene White, Sharon Wilkins, Ardania Williams, Bryan Williams, Dr. Jackie Williams, Julia Winbourne, Dr. Delores Winston, Leslie Witsett and Jim Wright. If I have forgotten anyone, please add your name:

Spirituality

Realities Of Life

Each day someone is born
healthy or disabled
but the gift of life
a joy to see
regardlessly each day someone dies,
sometimes tragic, biologically some kind of disease
maybe a heart attack
a departure from life
leaving loved ones saddened
a tear shed or some rejoicing for the life
of a journey to another place
a better place
not in the womb
hopefully to another world of eternity
if you believe
that the divine one died for your sins
as a baby,
you have to crawl before you walk
speak in a different tongue
babble the language
before perfecting words so clear
those around you
shape and mold you

Spirituality

you learn right from wrong
by doing, pursuing
learning from your mistakes
discipline, a must
showing love
not sparing the rod
a biblical verse
but correcting out of love
giving a spanking
years ago
was okay but
today no way
today you have to be careful
it's a new day, a new time
you can commit a crime
because of a law called child abuse
no more spanking
instead you have to talk
and redirect another mechanism of understanding
life has its ups and downs
some of us learn from our mistakes
some of us don't
some of us remain an uneducated fool
doing the same thing over again
we celebrate holidays, birthdays,
and new relationships too

Realities of Life

elated moments
we look at movies, TV
pictures that remind us
of yesterday
a job gained
a job lost
the haves, the have nots
vote to put the right one in office
don't vote
don't complain
if things change
and it's
not what you
wanted to remain
relationships unresolved
a break-up
a separation,
a divorce
maybe a war
robbing, killing
what sin?
soften your heart
love keeps no records of wrongs
severity of betrayal
a prayer for their salvation
influential in someone else's life

Spirituality

Poetry

poetry, it will take you
on an excursion
on a joy ride
while
listening to this poetry in motion
is a given
you see
it is spilling
a part of the spirit
from the soul
emptying like a well
of water flowing
at a pace
heavens gate
anyway
you want to take it
move it and let it flow
more than passing of time
poetry can even be given a rhyme
it's right on time
an expression from the heart
on each and everyone's part
sometimes a little tart

Realities of Life

it's an art
but the message always comes
every time the poetry is read
it has you thinking
and reminiscing
a different kind of fixing
a different kind of bread
reaching a new dimension
poetry, poetry
a message
a language
short but sweet
to the point
messages of poetry's
positivity, sensitivity
and sometimes some negativity
is keeping it real
in this world
of life's realities
that makes me feel blessed
experiencing
some of life's tests

Spirituality

Dream

My dream is as far as I can vision
and live it out,
like a ship
making it through the long choppy sea
no matter how rough,
how difficult,
keep pressing on
until you reach your destination
of a dream of
where you're going

Realities of Life

A Dream

A dream is a stream flowing,
within your memory
you have to catch it
while it's moving in the right direction,
like a wave of a tide
coming in,
staying alive with each thought
moving until it reaches its destination
of where it lays its final rest

A Feeling of Ease

when i pray
a sensation moves throughout my body
a warmth that rushes through me that soothes my soul
and calms my spirit
and puts it at ease
a comfort I can't explain
how good it feels
through his presence
nothing but joy
a smile that moves wildly across my face
you seem to always answer my prayers
in your time
through prayer there is never a worry
because you always take care of me
during difficult times
as well as my happiest moments
that's how great you are
near and far
always taking care of me
a feeling at ease
leaving me pleased

Realities of Life

A Love For Snow

Snowflakes lightly dropping
as the winter's breeze
pushes them around
dancing like deer galloping across the hills
surrounded by trees once dressed by leaves
sidewalks covered with snow
people shoveling their pavements to make a path
others building a snowman for hours
decorating with a scarf wrapped around the neck
adding eyes, a nose, a mouth, some ears
and some whiskers too
having so much fun
throwing a snowball
riding a sled down a hill
not minding a spill or two
not realizing how cold I've become
my fingers and feet become somewhat numb
it's time to end the outdoor fun
and go inside where warmth abides
and watch the snowflakes
from a window inside
while snowflakes fall

Spirituality

A Wake Up from You

a wake from you
six o'clock in the morning
a calm voice
sang out to me
music soft and sweet
a different kind
it got my attention
no more silence
the song so impressionable
sounds incredible
put my mind at peace
sending off releases of comfort
rhythmic strokes of octaves
strutting from extremes
giving diversity to your song
music not heard of often
a whistle of a few chirps
from your limb on the tree
I see you perched your sound
so great
others joined in
more serenity to my ears
a blend of a different sound

Realities of Life

Breaking Free

Breaking away, breaking free
from the bondage of sin
reciting to God
how thankful I am
for giving me a vision
of a light so clear
no longer lost
but found
full of sight
my spirit
is free
that you can believe
a peace within

Spirituality

Christmas Time

A celebration of the almighty one
Christmas time is a happy time
it's a day of great celebration
of the birth of Christ
who gave his life
to carry many generations more
oh what a joy
celebrating the miracle one

Realities of Life

Fashion Flair

I love to look fashionable
clothes a necessity
that's why I shop
for clothes, shoes, boots and sometimes a hat
sometimes i'm a bargain shopper
looking for a sale, looking for nice things
selecting carefully quality things
things that are interesting,
when wearing the fashions
i want to look grand
so that's the plan
wearing much color
like the color purple
even dark colors and plaids too
hats that will make you look twice
and say ooooooh i like that!
where did you get that?
so unique, so complete
even down to the manicured feet
wanting to give an image of me
from my head to my feet
caring about myself
that's why I shop

Spirituality

Girlfriends

When I walk into a room
visiting friends
my head is held high,
self respect I got for me
and it resounds with a smile
a word of hello given to everyone,
bouncing back to me
hello unresound
each friend a different smile,
a different personality
accepting what each one brings
one a great conversationalist
can stimulate your interest
and bring a shy one into the conversation
teaching a lesson every time,
elevating the mind all the time
another girlfriend stylish
always manicured from head to toe
hair always in place
with a little make-up on her face
neatly put into place
giving a glow of a natural look
clothes and shoes
another added dimension of style

Realities of Life

finesse of some success
teaching us lessons how to dress
an entrepreneur with a business sense
giving creativity how to make things
a home designer
helping us keep our personal best
always giving of yourself when advise is needed
telling another girlfriend to adjust the bra strap
to uplift the breast,
so she's not looking a mess
another girlfriend that sings like a bird
telling you like it is through her song
leaving room to bloom
a preaching sister, giving the word to pray
and let God have his way
to nurture the spirit to unrest
all of life's test
girlfriend a giver from the heart
a great supporter what ever the need
we laugh, we cry,
even bake each other
a cake to celebrate
a birthday, wedding, a promotion
a date, success at any state
girlfriend a heart worth gold to the soul

Spirituality

God's Gift

Sunrise, sunset, grass and trees
the sky with stars shining above
giving us brightness to shine below
on our lives a gift so rare
you have taken us to another hemisphere
children today were born yesterday
giving us a ray of their lives
out of darkness into brightness
unripe to ripeness
blossoming from the nutrients they are fed
love,
patience,
quality time
even through the
fun,
sun,
rain
and storms
all adorn the experiences of life,
where true learning begins,
and
never ends

Realities of Life

God Opened My Eyes

God opened my eyes to another way
of looking at things
like a huntsman focused on the game he wants to claim,
an aim for the perfect shot to hit its mark
and gain his flock
it's only a physical estate of the mind
full concentration, focused, fixated
I must thank God for staying with me
when I had fallen and thought that all was lost
at my cost taking to much time to stand on my own
spiritually lost, eyes closed, unable to see
what he had in blessing me
he miraculously picked me up, opened my eyes,
gave me a light, a scripture - Proverbs 4:7
Wisdom is the principal thing; therefore get wisdom
and with all thy getting, get understanding
this consumed me, it had a hold on my mind
can't shake him this time
devil don't have a chance
to take away my praise
He is in control of this dance
my soul, joyous, so sweet
a treat to set me free

Spirituality

He spoke to me and said,
through the difficult time, I want you to sow
spilling a tear drop, emptying my soul
a word so fulfilling of truth, love and peace,
making me whole keeping me still,
focused on God for sure
Proverbs 3:13
happy is the man that findeth wisdom and
the man that establishes understanding
not much left to misunderstanding
God healed me on the inside,
changing my mental estate before it became too late.
God opened my eyes wide!

Realities of Life

Gone A Little While
(dedicated to Robbie Carter & Kaliah Carter-Jones)

You left me today
but,
it's only for a little while
God lifted you up,
from
the
earth
to take you home,
a place called heaven,
where you're at peace,
at rest
living at its best,
with the king,
one day we will meet up again,
oh friend,
I'll be lifted up too
that's when the rejoicing will begin
to no end!

Spirituality

Healing

I got a visitation from God
it was awesome
I was sick
but I prayed and
He healed me

Realities of Life

It's Not Just My Agenda

Only God knows my agenda
he has all of my questions stored
and
all of my answers
to any problem
that I have
many times
I try to find my next destination
but,
I don't always go the route that I chose
it is not my decision alone
I ask for guidance from him
I then begin moving into directions
I never believed I could go in - which I traveled
But suddenly prior knowledge struck my mind
All things are possible
when
you focus on God

Spirituality

I Want To

i want to keep loving myself
as well as others
with self esteem running high
i take great pride
i want to be like salt and pepper
seasoned to add some flavor to
this humanistic character
my personality
maybe adding to another
i want to help the sales person
working for a commission
finding something i like
and buying it to help their cash flow
i want to still smile and shine like the sun
even when you don't want me to
cause i want to show love
and treat people right
it's like show and tell
and going outside with a child
and flying a kite
i want to mentor
and make a friend
i want to help a homeless person get a job

Realities of Life

something to eat,
some clean clothes,
a place to stay and off the street
doing it the united way
this is how it is supposed to be
to help in each and every way
finding your way back to the norm
in our society
full of proprieties
i want to help the sick
mental illness,
cancer and other diseases
with so much stress
depression on your mind
a mind that has gone astray
cause your body is in a different state
thinking about death
i know that you want to come back
and be aligned to your yesterdays
i want to talk with you,
help you with your fears
your drug addiction,
that has altered your thinking
and has you doing the wrong things
stealing, wheeling and dealing
i want to

Spirituality

give you encouragement
and tell you about the best plan
God is the one
who will set you free
this you gotta believe
try him you'll see
then you'll see your life change
completely
i want to
continue learning
and pass my learning on to others
so that they too can discover
what it is
that they want to uncover

Realities of Life

Just Pray

When things in life
upset you
unrest you
test you
get
the best of you
just stop
and
pray

Spirituality

Realities Of Life: Personal Quotes

- *Change comes when you don't want it to.*

- *Change happens unexpectedly.*

- *Change happens.*

- *There is always a blessing in the struggle.*

- *All of us have made poor choices and bad decisions. It's how we fix it that counts.*

Realities of Life

Seasons of Change

Seasons come and go
giving us much change
as experiences of life
there is an interconnection
with
heaven and earth
when we cry,
and
shed a tear
we release a drizzle of water
like the hemisphere
when our tears are heavily
falling,
it's like heavenly rain
releasing the tension
of
misunderstanding
when
happiness is no matter

Spirituality

Thanksgiving

Giving comes from the heart
when you give and share
you show that you care
a heart of gold hidden
but
showing brilliantly
the
beauty of your soul

Realities of Life

The Change

Oh how sweet the spring little flower
come out
be a daisy,
build a rose
and let your leaf be known
little flower
the warmth is over head now
go on
and flaunt the riches of your colors
so love the beauty you give
little flower
as your stem grows firm
and strong
oh little flower
the weather is taking its toll
watching your discolored leaves falling off
so as the wind blows mildly
and the ground hardens
and you inevitably grow old
I say,
farewell, little flower
for time
is life's control

Spirituality

Transformed By God

God is my transformer
He wakes a spirit inside of my heart
connecting my mind to all the elements of me
I'm alert on him
He is my friend
I'm focused to the end
while he's working within me
on the inside
I'm riding on the most high
feeling so free
open to him
blessings falling upon me
so openly
so free
between him and me
oh, I'm happy as I can be
for my light is shining brighter as the day goes by
because his love is on the inside
bringing forth much fruit on the outside
thankful to him
for my transformation

Realities of Life

Unsinned

Oh how beautiful the day begins
with a smile from you
I can't pretend
the way you make me feel unsinned
my soul so full of feeling that
I have just obtained a good friend
the glare of your sun's ray
shining so bright
coming together on a connective stare
we both openly want to share
so where do we go from here
conversation between us
so free
so full of care
talking long hours
into the night
with time not being a factor
just something we both like to do
oh how my interest is you

Spirituality

You Are The Source Of My Strength

You are my source of strength
you are my guide through the heavy rain
every time my spirit sings
its rhythmic style gives me sunshine
little rain
life has really changed
it's like night and day
revolving from darkness to light
taking me to another height
to a higher plane
oh, my spirit,
my spirit
my mind changed
no longer locked in chains
unlocking the past
what a class
removing the mask
doing the things that I want to now
I feel like Ms. America wearing a crown
walking so proud leadership abounds
now I'm walking so proud

Realities of Life

You Tried To Steal My Joy

I'm not going to let anyone
steal my joy
what
the good lord has stored
I must remember
some have not been taught
to treat people with kindness
but
when a scripture is read
it reminds us
who keeps us ahead

Spirituality

You Were Always There For Me

When I feel lonely and lose all hope,
you were there
when I cry and weep and can not sleep
you were there
watching over me when my faith is slipping away
you were there
uplifting like a car jack
lifting me up slowly
so that changing my damaged spirit
can be adjusted accordingly
taking away that damaged spirit
giving me a renewed one
when you are around
we can laugh, we can joke
and hold my interest to no end
you were there
to stroke my mind with your pleasurable sayings
slowly relaxing me
is the place
where I want to be
thank you
for helping
to bring the best out of me

Love

Love Is

Love is an extension of us
love is liking you
always improving ourselves
cultivating ourselves
as satisfying beings
love is giving to others
not only in need but
you just feel like
giving of yourself
so sincerely
love is thirsty
you always need to give
to keep you full and alive
love is a hug, an embrace, a touch
love is feeling good inside
Love is not having everything go your way
Love is tough but lasting

Realities of Life

To Love Someone

To love someone
is to be captured
by their very existence
to be tuned in to
all of their feelings
happy or sad
to accept them
as who they are unconditionally

Love

A Meeting A Thrill

What happened to us? Tell me do you know?
We were young and innocent when
your big brown eyes met mine
I became blind this was a sign,
my physical estate would not keep me straight.
I got this funny feeling in my chest, it just would not rest
it felt like juggling jello with my soul swerving rocking
and moving full of excitement, much confused
you see i never felt this way before – it is so new
i'm confused but i knew it meant something special
you spoke to me with that sweet, sweet voice
i felt the perspiration break out of my pores
i thought that i would plummet to the floor
i was so wet, i needed something to dry me up
in a quiet voice you said take my hand
puzzled for a moment, i asked
do i really want to take this stance,
it could easily turn into romance
i heard the voice again, i'd like to get to know you
again, i was somewhat puzzled, not quick to respond
but he made me feel at ease
I said, sure i am pleased, i'd like to get to know you too
we conversated, contemplated on where we should go
we don't know but i am willing to try
while we were blinded

Realities of Life

You Danced With Me

You wanted to dance with me
you got what you wanted
you danced with me with much persistence
of asking over and over again until you danced with me
and made my adrenaline rush
no, I won't fuss, it's feeling good right now
you didn't even know my name
you danced with me
we tangled with one another, got mangled
moving like a twisted chandelier
movement consumed with wind
my whole body screaming with satisfaction
my body absorbing much needed exercise
my nerves jumping
like a bouncing ball at a synchronized beat
my body bloomed with much excitement
no longer feeling depleted, my body got what it needed
a lost pound maybe two
sweat dripping as if I'd been in a shower
my clothes in combat, of wetness, a smell
a wash machine would welcome
but not until I'm done dancing with you
our moves compliment one another
glad you were persistent in asking me to dance with you

Love

Wonderful Thoughts Of You

Unconsciously, I have you on my mind
how do I know?
thoughts of you arrive, pictures keep surfacing
it has me thinking of you all of the time
is this because of your walk,
your smile, that charm i adore
it sticks to me like a thorn,
not a feeling of hurt,
but a feeling that will move me as soon as i am struck,
an alertness that perks me
it gives me a feeling of ecstasy
Your smile revives me, it involves me,
it captures the essence of my soul
my smile becomes automatic when yours reaches mine
oh how kind,
oh honey, you know your magic is so fine
your walk so swift and so smooth
i think you're cool
i love your charisma,
your parade, it's another phase
oh honey, it's hard for me to behave

Realities of Life

When I Am With You

When i'm with you, i feel so, so, so good
when walking and holding onto each other's hands
you see I never felt this way before
it's like feeling like a river moving slowly
quietly at peace with a riffle of a bend
of a hunk of sweat
carress every groove of our lifelines
in the palms of our hands
a sweet scent, a warmth sending no uneasiness
no unrest, our chests stroking together harmonically
dancing joyfully reaching every octave so naturally
as one
a feeling of one
happiness we have found
trust and comfort in each others arms
we have found happiness and joy in each other's hearts
we have found love that will last forever
the love I feel for you is strong and beautiful
it grows with each new day
overflowing my heart and bringing us together
and filling my heart and filling my life with all
the blessings of such a wonderful living
i love you

A Stare Of Surprise

You put a sparkle in my eye
your stare, your look
gave a deep message
upon contact
it stuck like glue
adhesive to paper
a reflection of a miracle
disguised
surprised
instantly
you filled my heart
with joy inside
you've given me
a gift
so precious and rare
giving my heart
a
tangle of a dance
a feeling so natural
a
whole new feeling within me
I'm happy to have met you

Realities of Life

My Prince Charming

I knew you were special from the very start
your gentle voice and your kind spoken words
the doors that you've held open for me
assisting me with taking off my coat
a stroke of your hand on my face and another place
putting me at ease, always feeling safe
with you always making me feel special
each and everyday
always doing something to give me a smile,
a dozen roses
an interesting conversation,
taking me out spontaneously for dinner
surprising me with a brand new dress,
so you can see my bright smile
all I can say is that you're one of a kind
although we've been together for some time
you have kept our relationship at its best
so fresh
giving me phone calls throughout the day
oh, I never knew love could be this way
until I met you
and
you came my way

Love

You Are Unreal

You are the love
I thought I'd never see
How could this be
A dream maybe
A dream made me see
Oh how wonderful life could be
You danced around in my head
and gave my heart and soul
a rush
right out of bed
now I'm running around the house
singing, dancing
boy you,
make me feel so good inside
like no other could
your gentleness of a kind word
spoken
so sound
so sweet
Oh how you seep into me
like grits hot off of a plate
a rising a meeting of such good taste
now I know my place with you
a dream that became a part of you and me

Realities of Life

Wedding Day

Today is our day
my love
I give to you
a commitment we make
to one another today
a day we become one
a look into each other's eyes
focusing on our prize
a smile upon your face mirrors mine
so blessed,
to have you enter my life today
we pledge our love to each other
in a special way
a tear sheds
feeling so much joy
reciting our vows
a gift of rings
we give to one another
a symbol of our love
a seal of a kiss
to show our love
and affection
on our special day

A Kiss of a Different Kind

A kiss of a different kind
I thought that I was going to lose my mind
a kiss given to me by my friend journeyed downward
in a slow spiral from the side of my cheek
gently placing soft big lips into another spot
hunting for more game, slowly moving, gently lifting
and placing the lips down again
a wetness I could now feel
not just lips, a tip of a tongue emerged through its home
making its run, gently stroking
making a splash, a continuous flow of wetness unfolds
a hot flash arises like wearing a warm fur
my soul obliges, can't fight the feeling
enjoying what it brings, feeling good
the lips healing me reaches a new destination
it meets its match, another home, a set of lips
waiting to capture the feeling it felt on the cheek
it makes me want to sing oh weee weeeeee
lips touch gently kissing slowly
a tongue emerges through its home to visit another,
opening the canal wiggling, scurrying like a fish
that fell out of a dish, slowly wiggling tongues
join the rapture of moving up, down, all around,
stroking to a place of satisfaction, both tongues,
much reaction to an attraction

Realities of Life

Feeling You

We lay here
just enjoying the vibe
just feeling the vibe
of being in the presence
of one another
feeling the warmth of radiation
of heat coming from our bodies
from underneath a cover
feeling you without a touch,
a look from you
feeling me
but suddenly
everything changes
our eyes talking to each other
on a connective stare
telling us to move
a little bit closer
to one another
an arm finally meets
its destination
of wrapping around my body
still moving towards one another
until we interlock

Love

like a nut to a bolt
i can feel your breath
like a warm summer night
almost a perfect degree of air
making contact
with my bare skin erupting
my blood flows within
elevating every stem, every limb
now my organs are moving, thriving
no, i'm not jiving
i'm feeling the vibe of you
inside my spirit
you got a hold of my emotions
i'll let my heart be my guide
do what it feels,
it's pulsating like a roaring engine
all of a sudden my feelings
i can't hide
my heart is in override
it will tell me what to do
before we make the next move
is that cool, you whisper
i whisper something, we kiss
now we have something
 to reminisce
isn't that bliss

Realities of Life

Unconditionally Love

You look at me just staring
and
of course
I stare back
when there is something
that needs attention
you let me know
by asking
and
I fulfill
your need
even when
I
don't want to
or
feel
like it but
I do it
cause
I want to
cause
you've been
so good to me

Love

You

Your smile means so much to me
all the things i need are found
i can't count the happy times
that you and i shared
i can't count the many ways
you've showed me that you cared
i can't count my loving thoughts
so many, i lost count
but just as long as memories last
and wishes still come true
my deepest thoughts will continue
to be "i love you"

Realities of Life

Your Opened and Closed Spirit

Why are you so quiet? why are you so mad?
has life been so bad? is this why you are sad?
i tried to talk with you but you would not let me in
why not listen
you don't realize what you're missing
i'm not giving up
i'm going to try again
i'm talking to you again
when are you going to begin?
you don't have to stay mad
i can turn your sadness, your madness to gladness
i can put a smile on your face
i can make you laugh
now are you ready to talk to me?
i don't have to think again
i'll talk to you again
this time you'll talk back
i'll ask a question then you will respond
i knew you would talk this time
because I made you feel
good inside
i knew you could talk
all of the time

Runaway Love

You're no longer giving me
the attention that you once gave
an adoration
I loved only from you
you exclusively gave me
all of your attention
I'm no longer getting
instead you went astray
constantly around another
giving your laughter
your conversations
you once shared with me
you flaunted yourself
with the opposite gender
using your charisma
giving them your emotional flair
talking about the drama in your life
accepting others' opinions
changing your thoughts
your behavior
instead of
trying to talk about it
with your significant other

Realities of Life

you're not bringing anything to the table
with me no more
the emotional piece is missing
maybe boredom
for being together for so long
taking me for granted
we had a relationship
that once was
well planted
I thought I still ignited your fire
set your heart ablaze
now
I find myself in maze
not knowing where to go
I'll find my way out
without a doubt
and
then
I'll know
where I'm going

Love

I Enjoyed Your Company

I was invited by a friend to visit their home
to my surprise
a visitor was there
we were introduced
without a boost
conversations between us began
we sampled some foods
drank some wine
of good beer
we talked like
we knew each other for years
I poured on the charm
no reason for anyone to be alarmed
it's nothing serious
just curious about the excitement
of the conversation that you give
after you left
you made an impressionable effect
so my friend followed up with a phone call
and put me on the phone
I stated,
I enjoyed your company
my response,
I did too

Realities of Life

is this a start of something new,
I believe my friends
are trying to hook me up
with someone new,
I enjoyed the company,
just a super time,
conversation at its best
but nothing more
just that I enjoyed
the conversation
at best

An Affair

You are married but committed to another
a sin committed indeed
why bother
what made you stray?
so you roamed and
found someone to fulfill your needs
now i guess you're pleased
so you found someone else to talk with you,
take a walk with you, take your hand
your whole life has a new plan

don't you know having an affair
is no solution to the problem
Why bother!
Don't you know that you are a form of recreation
play, you are having a grand time
flirting, wining and dining
enjoying life in your mid-life crisis
how long do you think this will last?
after spending much time with your new found love
after awhile your consciousness begins to bother you
after awhile you're hearing some of the same character
qualities of your significant other in this new found love
causing much strife inside your heart and mind

Realities of Life

your emotions start playing you
your soul is under construction
before realizing that you miss your significant other
now you have feelings of wanting to rediscover
a relationship once lost
all that was so bad
is not so bad within your thoughts no more
do you stay married, or committed to another
only your heart can deliver the matter

Love

A Relationship Gone Bad

When I spoke to you
you did not speak back
I can't continue this relationship
with
your unfriendly characteristics
hoping that you'll change
a spirit within me
said
no way
no communication
the emptiness inside
I can't hide this is not a part of me
I gotta go, gotta move on
I know its not going to be easy
for
me
but
I'll adjust some kind of way
my life is on its way
to a complete change

Realities of Life

Why You Want To Act Like That

We were once one
giving so much love
having so much fun
our circumstances changed
things became undone
you were away from me
for awhile
with much distance between us
your mind became consumed with negativity
poisoned, leading to distrust
misunderstandings
cause you're accusing
cause you're assuming
you have no real facts
why do you want to act like that
cause tension like that
can't break
can't shake
living in the past
nothing that deals with this present relationship
why are you thinking like that
is it instability?
if not insecurity?

Love

you need to stop interpreting things untrue
full of misunderstanding
how can you be true
to someone who loves you?
why act like that
making me feel blue
why block the love
i'm beginning to feel a sense of rejection
where is the love and affection
your misunderstandings
are just an illusion
your gut feelings
running on emotion
it's only a notion
if your perception does not change
my love will not remain the same
can't stand the pain
my heart crying tears
like a sprinkler letting water flow
where is that old compassionate heart
if you don't change
we'll have to depart
like a working piece of art
moving in different directions
i'm older
smarter, wiser now

Realities of Life

i think differently now
not that naive person that you use to know
i'm letting things flow
what ever will be so
believe me
you will know

Anger

Why are you so angry?
who has made you mad?
What are your real issues
it's obvious that they're unresolved
because you explode
like an eruption of a volcano
you come out a different kind of mold
reciting things of the past
when in an argument
you still won't let go
of your locked up soul
with that old harbored stuff
not connecting with me
always fighting
you gotta let go
of the negativity eating at your soul
eroding, needing a fix
to restore, to calm down
anger going now

Realities of Life

My Tears

My tears are falling again
why?
problems in a relationship
another relationship break-up
i'm believing that this is the end
you won't let go of the past
accusing me of things to no end
making false accusations
is this because of your own digressions
maybe this is how you're living
don't try and put a guilt trip on me
cause, I no longer have blinders on
you see
i'm older now,
much, oh much wiser
I know circumstances have changed this relationship
the trust is a question mark
now the relationship can not thrust
cause you're holding on to unwanted stuff
within your mind
locked in chains unable to move
unable to think clearly now
that's what's wrong with this relationship
how long will this last?

Love

A Heart Once Captured

If you could go back
when your head was in my heart
you knew the real me
you would stroke me with your sweet talk
and tell me how much you cared
you know that I still love you
but your love has changed
you're playing a different ball game,
your heart is not at home
instead it has gone foul many times
moving in the wrong direction
what will it take for you to reach home
and make contact with every base
so that you can make it home without an out
It's evident that you need much practice
because you have drifted many times in the outfield
your emotions showing frustration everywhere
the temper flaring like a balloon letting out hot air
that's not fair
you have much sun glare
blocking the brightness that was once there
someone who once cared
so sincere

Realities of Life

You're Not The Perfect One

You're not the perfect one
please take me as I am
with all my wrongs unconditionally
I'm still in love with you
You gotta believe but
this argument we had was so different
like no other before
you blurted out things
without thinking
your tongue became a weapon
saying things that stuck
like grits cooking
so hot
in a crock pot
cooking too long
bubbling hot
scorching, wounding my spirit
altering my thoughts about you
it's gonna take much from you
to change my spirit
back to where it lived before
after time has passed
it's something realized

Love

I Want Sunshine Too

I have lived for your vision
your dreams
the sun can't shine
all the time
in your life
you gotta make an adjustment
to mine
and
let me have some sunshine
and
do the things I like to
just like you

Realities of Life

Love

Love
a ripple of a notion
of the heart,
speaking fluently,
like a seasonal change
happiness shines brightly,
elevating to the highest peak,
a release of eruptions of what's within
unexplainable sensations
of the soul memories of the past
of pain that lies within
like a door that closes to darkness
but
a door opens again
shining a new light
love comes again
a renewal of happiness
gives another insight
of love, a taste of blends,
a flavor of a choice
how love will end

Love

You Were There

You were the one
I thought I never find
But there you were
standing right
in front of me
lonely standing there
standing there
all by yourself
you turned around
and
you
looked at me
with
a
smile

Realities of Life

No Longer A Friend

Never a problem with a friend until you
you were my friend
someone I thought I knew
we were inseparable
talking to one another everyday
often I helped you whenever
there was a need
in every way
so what happened
you broke the trust
you see
you embarrassed me
more than once
in front
of a group of people
why
cause you want to control things
your way
I don't have time to play games
and of course
I expressed how I felt
but you took it to heart
hardening of your heart

Love

a place that's operating
like a fuse blown
not knowing how to turn on the light
and realize that this phase of misbehavior
not a good flavor
so soften the heart
so it can pump some love
getting your revenge
stripping me of my reign
cause of your selfish gain
you broke the trust
a bond no longer stands
no longer comfortable with you
misleading me with your half-truths
manipulating controlling ways
jealousy
you have something
I never saw long ago
tell me
what's going on with you
who's influencing you?
you want to take ownership of
everything that's not yours
why is it that
you don't want
to see me blessed!

Realities of Life

You Taught Me Lessons The Hard Way

You taught me lessons the hard way
but I thank you
because of it, i'm a stronger person
because of it, you opened my eyes to a world
i thought i'd never see
so much history
of you hiding yourself
wearing a disguise
I never knew much mystery until
you lifted those hidden blinders
not showing the real you
you taught me lessons the hard way
I see
I saw
the other side of you
you came out
no longer wearing a disguise
I was surprised
to see how you begin living
playing games with me
getting mad with me
stopping the conversation
stone cold

Love

not apologizing
for your actions
it's just a fraction
of showing who you really are
you're not the same
you have changed
trying your power moves
and
controlling moves
trying to force total control
you're not the same
because of it, i'm a stronger person
moving to another level
you taught me lessons the hard way

Realities of Life

This Weight Is A Problem

You know this weight is a problem when
you can't fit your clothes
can't touch your toes
and a bulge unfolds
outside of the sleeve
your belly,
even below the knee
it showed a bulge
the morning you met me
you know you got a weight problem
when you keep bringing it up
talking about your unwanted fat
gotta lose some weight
but instead
eating fried chicken
on top of all of that
feet hurting
back hurting
hands and arms too
your weight is tired too
of you singing the blues
not taking a walk
no ***exercise!***

Love

Mental Equation

I'm sitting here relaxing,
my mental estate working within
which direction will I go
a light turns on within me
thinking about yesterday,
today, tomorrow
where will I go
and what will I do
after evaluating,
moving as the world turns
and changes of things come about
equating a vision
then the desire of my mental estate
becomes much clearer
goals come into play
a time
a order
things become set

Realities of Life

Music

Music is so soothing to my soul,
Jazz so improvised
it will make you rise
and
tap your feet
and not skip
a beat
shake like a wondering leaf,
instruments of many kinds
holding my ears captive sometimes,
eyes closed meditating, feeling the vibe
of
many vibrations inside,
so smooth, so cool
relaxing me,
my mind taking in the sounds
meditating,
giving what it brings
my heart sings
at its best
no regression
just succession
of
good sounds

Love

What Makes Me Happy

Taking care of me
that's how life should be
leaving me content
a warm reading, a bubble bath, a good book,
dim light candles lit around me
putting me in a relaxed mood
soothing my soul
with God involved
focusing on the positive word
I begin to think sweet serenity
all the possibilities for me uncovered
my mind, my body, my physical estate
now I am equipped
to be care free
at peace with my spirit as well as others
to give a smile, a hug, a tear, a laugh, a dance
all the possibilities of me uncovered
that has been discovered

Realities of Life

Inspire

You are the captive one of my soul
you make me feel so whole
with your instruction
that motivates me
to exceed
excel to a level
of boldness
of completion desired

Loving Self

When you love you
you can't do any better

Don't let someone influence you
to do the wrong thing
when you know
the right thing to do

The light is not out
until I'm ready

Don't blame others
for your ignorance
explore your self

If it's not working
find something that will

If I am distant
guess who moved

Honor and Cherish

Honor and Cherish

Mother

A mother is a special gift
sent from heaven above
to bless me
throughout my life
with
her continuous love
gifts
giving of herself
unconditionally
a gift to treasure
for
many years to come
within
my heart always
and
forever

Realities of Life

Father

Father you are quite a role model
you call me your angel
you tell me that I'm pretty,
and
a smart one too
oh, how special you make me feel
your guidance I accept openly
reading to me,
almost everyday
filling me with your knowledge,
leading me toward the right path
tucking me into bed
giving me a hug,
a kiss,
a saying,
a prayer
and
then
good night
I love you

Grandmothers

A Grandmother's love is like a gem
always letting you sparkle
in whatever you do

Realities of Life

Sisters

Sisters, "**I love you**"
we are women of distinction
always carrying ourselves as honorable mention
we share so much in common
a conversation full of excitement
a laugh or two, a hurt, a pain
when we disagree, we are still care free
you're never easy to anger
never any underhanded games for selfish gain
sincerely a bond desirably shared
no one can shake or move
always showing that we care
with helping others in need
community service, a good deed
with much respect given, much love shown
trust never a question
a characteristic well known

***S**incere*
***I**ntelligent*
***S**upportive*
***T**ruthful*
***E**xceptional*
***R**elationships*

Honor and Cherish

Elders, We Thank You

Elders, we honor you
for your wisdom viable today
your age has added a new dimension
through your life experiences
you're like wine that ages
you get better as time passes by
you have so much to share
with the young as well as the old
you tell stories of your past and present life
your stories begin to unfold so naturally
not realizing the impact you have on our lives
you teach to each one of us lessons learned
you open our eyes to the whole new world
helping us to explore,
the destination that we have not yet traveled
you're navigating us to another place
helping us to make the right choices
before we arrive at our destination
thank you elders for showing us pride,
and sharing with us your past trials
tribulations, the good with the bad but
most of all, thanks for the love you have shown
your care, your concern for helping us to learn

Realities of Life

A Death Of A Loved One

Death is a transition
that all of us must face
the trauma of death
of the human race
oh,
it hurts us inside
our hearts flourish
with running water
that spills into our soul
our eyes filled
with a pocket
of a tear
we are at a loss
hurting inside wondering why
but within time
we slowly heal
the master holds us in his arms
helping us to bare the loss
of
a loved one
assuring that our loved one
is in
a better resting place
as we mourn

Aunt

A aunt is a special part of me
she is always showing that she cares
with
a compliment of encouragement
lending an ear
when problems arises
giving advice,
always nice
a love so warm

Realities of Life

Children of Innocence

Children, Children, how special you are…….
your precious presence of innocence so premature
wanting to learn
your eyes so wide,
they sparkle so clear……..
your ears so tentative
they perk without fear
taking information from others
sometimes it's like fitting pieces to a puzzle
taking the time to sort things through
and
remembering what you need to know
keep on doing what your doing
until you reach
your
goal
you'll be okay
it will take a little time
until you reach your prime,
and have a life like mine
one of a kind

Delivery

We are eagerly
waiting for you to arrive, baby
can't wait for the blessings of birth
upon our eyes
when you enter the world
you may enter with a loud cry
or kick your feet,
move your arms,
your legs
or move those eyes
to see what's around you
maybe even bare a smile
family and friends meet
to greet you with open arms
awaiting to talk with you
staring at you (thankful for the gift of life)
adore you,
cherish you,
care for you
and pray for you
showing much love for you
a gift of life
life for you begins
within the extended family

Realities of Life

Friendship Is A Gift

Having a friend is a special gift
someone who gives you their heart
a different kind of beat
that
you can appreciate
because
a
friend always shows
how much they care
by
respecting you,
never embarrassing you
helping when a need arises
giving a listening ear
always there full of surprises
telling their stories of sharing a laugh or two
discussing things
whether you agree
or disagree
loving you unconditionally

Give To Oneself

Children you came to school to learn
all the lessons taught to you
by
a teacher
a friend
one precious gift
you can give to oneself
a benefit that will last a lifetime

Realities of Life

Mentor

You are the leader I follow
For you teach me well
a smile
a kind word unfold
showing me the operations of work
the do's and don'ts
helping to mold the right skill
until a reprint of likeness unfolds
following in your footsteps
Mentor,
you are gold

Honor and Cherish

Our Wedding Day

Our big day is here
oh, we waited for this day
for oh so long,
today our lives will change
we will never be the same
our lives will change
we're making this big commitment
becoming one, showing our love
your eyes connecting with mine
reciting our vows, a spoken word of love
exchanging rings
showing our symbol of love for all to see
our rings that shines
that keep us bind
a kiss no one can take away
the love we share
so memorable, so clear
locked in our memory
a time to cherish
a new life
a new beginning on
our wedding day

Realities of Life

Rememberance

Mom, "I Love You"
I remember the pretty dresses
you brought for me
and sewed for me to wear
you placed pretty bows
and ribbons in my hair
you treated my sisters and me fair
always a kind word
a hug
a kiss
showed you cared
giving advice
trying to direct the right path
in which road I should travel
my years with you were wonderful
a blessing i've realized
you brought much love and happiness
a blessing
always joined by love
all because
you know
how to love

Honor and Cherish

Special One

Children with special needs
you were born with a disability
but
your smile is so wonderfully made
a gentle spirit that you convey
an appreciation of giving
and
receiving from another
giving those around you joy
from
your sunshine face,
your arms that extend
to show love
a jubilation of laughter
arriving from within
patience that adorns
you bring a different order to life

Realities of Life

Teacher

A teacher is a gift to us all
always preparing lessons
with the goal in developing achievement
teaching lessons
helping the mind to grow intelligently
helping children to believe in themselves
inside, outside, an action shown
building self esteem
a kind word,
sometimes a scold, a direction
a pat on the back,
giving of encouragement
bringing joy to their lives
helping them to perform
to reach their potential
their capacity for greatness

Honor and Cherish

Thank You Mary McLeod Bethune

You unselfishly sacrificed your life giving to others
building a college so Negroes could learn
you showed great concern
for their educational needs
always striving, helping others to succeed
always exhibiting the spirit of the Lord
telling us that God inspired you to keep us focused
you founded and gave us
"The National Council of Negro Women"

Thank you for investing in us
giving us a vision of faith, courage, ambition and
dignity to rid ourselves of things that separate us
with the intention of keeping us apart
always instructing us to help others,
when they have lost their way,
guiding or leading them to the right path
you built an organization
so that we can lead others,
and help others be leaders of tomorrow
your philosophy has taught
and nourished us
you have touched our lives in a special way
more than what words can explain

Realities of Life

we know that your spirit lives within us
you are an angel, smiling down on us,
shedding light, spreading much love
we will continue to live out
your last will and testament
your legacy we will truly
carry on

Honor and Cherish

When I Think About You

When I think of you it's about your loving way
it's truly a blessing what God has made
you are full of joy, so happy so free
you have been an angel sent to me
When loving you, my heart flutters
when you speak to me
I hear no other
it's hard to disagree,
cause you're always trying to please
so unconditionally
I am mesmerized by your sweetness
always a kind word, a gentle touch
your wondrous radiant smile
it ignites my spirit to a marvelous light
it gives me much joy and inspiration
I think of you when I pray everyday
and asked God
to send someone like you my way
I give thanks to the Almighty
who answered my prayers
with great care
for sending you my way

Society

THE TWIN TOWERS, NYC
Illustration by Nedra Lowery (Age 16)

Realities of Life

911

A terrorist act
A plane out of control, well planned
One tower hit
and
then another
to unfold our Twin Towers
Our many countries of power
but in the attack
you accomplished a senseless act,
but we will survive
united as one
we will never run
we have God as our power
we are all a part of the Twin Towers

Society

A Bus Ride Home

I stepped onto a bus full of people
finding a place to stand
it was not grand
with no open space
people packed like sardines
with no place to move
a smell not refreshing
so many lively bodies
sweating on a very hot summer day
the air conditioning not giving the coolness
it should bring
i continued to walk
until someone decided to make some space
and move asideso I could slip in
i said thank you and stood within the little space
that i was given
i stood sideways for the duration of the ride
while holding onto the upper guard rail
a young teenager stood on the right side of me
a complete stranger
i felt this stranger would feel comfortable
if I spoke their generational slang
so instead of staring into space
i struck a conversation

Realities of Life

i said, what's up?
the stranger looked at me oddly
not realizing that I was using slang
he replied, the sun was up so high
in the sky today shining brightly
my eyes were affected by the sun's glare
it was obvious that this stranger did not have a clue
as to what I was talking about
my meaning of what's up
i replied back
yea, that sun was up high yesterday!
he surprised me
by saying what's up to me
trying to please me by using the same language
what's up with you?
i'm about to teach him something new
about my philosophy of slang
i told the story of when I said "what's up" to a friend
my friend in turn replied what's up to me
the stranger quickly learned
another definition of the word
it means hello and
I learned another interpretation
taken to a new awakening
a new awakening for us two

Society

A Changing World

War, a major threat to peace
since 911 the world has changed
and caused you so much emotional pain
are we near our last day in time?

the world is under global uneasiness
with terrorist attacks being a threat
with new technology
countries building weapons
of mass destruction
just to strengthen a nation
with arsenal and nuclear weapons
it's only a matter of time
that we will have sophisticated weapons
available that are capable of reaching distant targets
in another land,
wearing face masks would be the ultimate plan
uncertainty of being struck by chemical weapons
are we living near our last day in time?

we are living in a dangerous place
with much heightened security
in airports, public buildings,
homes and schools are even at risk
it's not an illusion

Realities of Life

seeing scenes of destruction
from our enemies on TV
the result of people living in fear
locked in our memory
watching people escape so narrowly
from losing their lives
while others die
are we living in our last day and time?

we are no longer feeling safe
all of our occurrences have shaken our lives
leaving us with emotional scars
our sense of security lost
how do we change the cause?
by uniting for peace

Society

A Day Erased

Oh, Philly, there were problems on Osage
middle class people just trying to live
enjoy life and take pride in where they live
but their day abruptly came to a stop
police and fire trucks all around
who would have thought such tragedy would hit
this middle class neighborhood
a bomb dropped to give a scare
but instead a fire flared out of control
on one home to drive a family out
who barricaded themselves
within for what they believed in
now the suffering begins for families
fire spreading to other homes
burning fire spreading
to another block over to Pine
burning a block of homes
all gone, no longer with a home
many roam to another place called home
a relative's home, Red Cross, maybe a room,
an apartment, a temporary place,
now looking at the aftermaths of it all
an unbelievable sight for a scene in America
it was like looking at TV

Realities of Life

it was like looking at TV
from scenes of Beirut
you gotta erase this chapter
pray and be thankful
for your life
getting out
gotta move on
starting fresh
healing starting
over again

Society

A Job

I got the job
a new adjustment
new people to meet
to become familiar with
and
work towards being a team player
listening to others
attending meetings
offering my suggestions
collectively finding solutions
reading memos
copying demos
demonstrating my leadership skills
in every sector of the job
communicating effectively
a promotion in order
soon
or
later
i got the job learned
moving to another level
exposed
polished

Realities of Life

A Rapid Changing World

We are living in a rapidly changing world.
Our children all over our country
are dying on the street not by their account but
we are living in a world that is rapidly changing.
Girls, boys, playing with friends
can easily get hit by gun fire
destroying us with hurt, anger and pain
this is the world were living in now,
not like the days of yesterday year
a version of reality politics and old time religion
with a vision much clearer
but living today
you're not the same
your history is another game
there is so much anger
families left in grief
a young girl with so much promise
was offered drugs and became hooked
unable to pay her debt, stabbed to death
so young, so smart
her future cut short
a mother's devastation
some people don't care anymore about helping one
another confusion

Society

what an illusion
TV cartoons full of violence
our children are learning so young
how to become violent
we gotta feed them the proper message
like an Olympic gold Medalist
running with the torch of fire
so proud for being recognized
for being the best at their game
but now were living with jealousy, drugs,
the uneducated, not enough money
our youth identify
with wearing the expensive clothes, tennis shoes
trying to keep up with the "Jones"
parents living beyond their means
trying to please
money wasted
with money you don't have to try to impress
much that could have been invested
money saved for a rainy day
for a house, a car, an education, even a vacation
to a place afar
with rapid changes in our society
we have to look at our priorities
and help each other to become a better society
in this rapid changing world

Realities of Life

Choices

There is so much that this world gives us
we live in a world full of struggles
a world changing quickly
with violence, robbery, drugs, HIV, unemployment
the employed learning from experiences
from a mother, father, teacher or a friend
the TV can teach us much
cause the bad guy
gets caught
and never wins

Society

Crime

Crime is happening everyday
someone robbed, maybe shot to death
the victim of the crime has lost all sense of happiness
and now becomes stressed
by the motives so senseless, so dumb
someone not caring for another or acting as one

oh help me sister, help me brother
I am unemployed, a gun is my new found toy
to take an opportunity, some money
maybe some jewelry
or help me to unfold the debt that I'm in
gotta buy food and clothes
a roof over my head
to sleep in a bed
so my babies can be fed

i know what i'm doing is not right
i'm desperate
hoping i don't get caught
all i need is someone to help
to keep my head leveled
a little help
a little direction
to help me live right

Realities of Life

Driving

Driving, sometimes a pleasure
on a highway in a city
a dirt road or a paved one
but more economics for the family are needed
today more people are traveling to work
more cars on the highways and byways
traffic moving fast
gotta be alert
gotta be a smart driver
and look out for the reckless one
you don't want an accident to happen
a damaged car
an injury

driving can be a pleasure
much scenery to see
so much beauty
such as birds, colored leaves on trees,
seeing the beauty
of rivers, oceans and moving seas

driving takes you
where you want to go

Society

Education Is A Tool

Education is an important tool
to have as your resume
to move ahead
no time to miss school
so get involved
in positive things
join a school activity
homework is important too
unable to do the work
ask a teacher, a mentor or a friend
try to do your best
don't settle for less
you can pass many tests
and when you graduate
maybe go to college
or learn a skill
and become educated
polished
with an intelligent mind
you can get a good paying job
and maybe someday
become one of the best
scholars in the nation

Realities of Life

In The Congo

In the Congo
life is dark for me
shady men
invade my mental estate
endangering permanence
of altering my mind
to places I do not wish to go
but,
I have no control,
the brutal enforcement
of bodily contact made upon my skin,
the pain enraged my spirit
a part of me lost emotionally
where do I began
to
fulfill my life again,
open up,
be happy,
maybe some prayers,
or help from the unknown
that will give an answer,
a direction,
a healing
to my characteristic estate

Society

Leadership

You are my leader
for you hold all the right substances
because you are full of valuables,
that contains the contents of all the right characteristics
of a well rounded person
your willingness to help and guide me in any endeavor
this is why I emulate you

your gentle smile is infectious,
contagious it brings a smile back and warms the heart
this is why I emulate you

your positive spoken words of encouragement,
your honesty and your constructive criticism
you always enlighten me to a new way
of looking at things through
the communication that we share
this is why I emulate you

you are giving to others
always willing to help when someone is in great need
to guide with great pride
this is why I emulate you

you took me under your wing unselfishly
as to how to conduct my behavior

Realities of Life

my choice of words
that are so enlightening
nothing you've given was forgotten
thank you for all that you do
this is why I am fond of you
I love you!

Leadership Qualities

Watch your character because what people see and hear is what they believe is a part of you.

Watch your habits - they become your practice.

Watch your practice - make sure that this is what you want to master.

Watch your body language and be conscious of what messages you are sending to others.

Watch your kindness - it can make a difference in how people treat you.

Realities of Life

Money

We all who work get what we earn
money
money that comes in many colors
green, brown, gold silver and copper
a make-up of paper
a make-up of coins
to use for our buying power
to buy some groceries
pay some bills or go to a restaurant
and buy a meal
keep on the lights in the home
so you can model in the mirror, comb your hair
money can buy you a trip to Rome
by boat, plane or train
money can buy you a car, furniture
money can have you sing the blues
so much money spent
oh did you forget to pay your 10% tithe
that will come back to you as time passes by
money can change you
give you power
any hour
control what you want
some people can buy an election

Society

can even buy affection
of another
wine and dine
money can buy into organizational crime
controlling business establishments
slots, prostitution
money you can lose
a bad investment can leave you in a crunch
not having enough to pay your bills
your debt impacting your credit
unable to buy some lunch
leave you in a crunch

Realities of Life

The New Generation

Times have changed for you
you live in a society full of promise
but yet it's hard to stay young and innocent
as the older generation once knew
New Generation
this world is giving you so much to see
such as drugs, TV, violence and sexual activity
with all of this you are living life's real realities
New Generation
you are growing up too soon
so much for your young mind to consume
like a flower budding so fast
unable to blossom slowly
to appreciate its growth of each stem
opening at a fast pace
dying so soon
New Generation
your ears endure alot too
so much profanity and not enough clarity
of what life should be
shown by actions of a different society
how much harm has this present society caused you?
many male artists surrounded by women
being caressed by them

Society

touched by them
television commercials that tease,
and seduce our minds
showing near sexual encounters
that only the blind can't see
what kind of messages are we sending
to our young,
eyes and minds
what you see
is the more
you have
the better it is
is this smart?
no it's not
do you know about HIV, AIDS, an awful disease?
producing a baby without protection,
a pregnancy not planned can happen so easily
sexual activity that can lead to disease
and have you displeased
feeling a lot of heartache and pain
ask yourself
why am I putting my life in danger?
this is insane
just to satisfy an urgency of pleasure with no protection
you better put an umbrella on the apparatus
and protect what matters
still a child yourself

Realities of Life

no money, no plan
don't rob yourself of your childhood reign
New Generation
wake up
some of you want to earn lots of money so fast
so quick so you can possess
the expensive material things that you desire
not honestly
selling drugs will make you holler
living your life so dangerously
always looking over your shoulder
so uncomfortably
you really don't want to go to jail
and live life once thought of as a fairy tale
New Generation
get your education
it is the key to your success
focus on what your parents, teachers
and loved ones say
you soon will be on your way
to a place of knowing what right
success awaits what's right
success awaits you despite the odds

What Is Leadership?

Leadership is the ability to lead others and self.

You lead others by influences that are acquired from being around others whom have been successful.

You need a purpose and the willingness to help others. You need to have an inner hunger to help others.

Having the right attitude is important. **Are you able to keep a positive attitude under adverse circumstances? Good!**

No matter what obstacles that you come up against, you have to have the willingness to keep pressing on and holding on to your dream. You will come up against people who are not kind and don't want you to succeed.

When people become jealous they lie; they become rude and nasty. They offer you their support and then when you call on them they withdraw the support originally offered to you.

You have to keep yourself motivated through all of this. You have to surround yourself with people who are in leadership positions and learn from their experiences.

When someone has angered you in your place of work, within an organization, or at a meeting and has not treated you fairly, do not become vengeful and let them stifle you

Realities of Life

in getting ahead. You can rest assure that through their devilment, they will move on while you are still holding on being angry. You have to empty your mind of the negatives and visualize doing so.

Get motivated! Be a doer! Move forward. Do an outstanding job at whatever you are involved in. People hold on to guilt. Some people can say the wrong thing and have us so upset that we become defensive. Remember that you can think positively and say to yourself, "I will not put up with this negativity. I know that I am a beautiful person."

Empower ourselves with our own uniqueness. This is our capacity for greatness.

You have to let go of the past memories that were not good for you and stop getting emotional.

Inspire - Inspiration plays a big part in becoming a leader. Through inspiration, you can help change someone's thoughts and behavior.

Encourage - Be innovative, be creative. When things go wrong, the only thing that will keep you moving is a strong drive to continue to lead no matter what the circumstances are. Say a kind word and give to others.

Motivate - You have to be hungry for what you want to do and believe that you can achieve the goals you have set for yourself. Surround yourself with positive people

Society

set for yourself. Surround yourself with positive people that will help you become successful. Read positive books and attended educational events.

Activate - Only you can decide if you can achieve your goals. Only you can do so by beginning the race.

Leadership you must exemplify your purpose and have a vision of your life.

Ask yourself where are you going? What is your goal?

Leadership - Everyone has leadership skills but it depends on your concept of what is leadership.

Leadership - Everyone has a unique way of presenting their skills.

Leadership skills - You must know who you are. You must know your strengths and weaknesses and how to assess them. Get your education by reading or through other resources. When you include spirituality in your life, you can withstand anything that comes your way.

Realities of Life

Katrina

nature's devastation to the land
the sky lightened gradually turned gray
like a painters brush stroking and forming an image
of what it wants the eye to see
a mood of a change of a portrait
a drop of rain flows from the darkened shy
it picks up its pace falling heavily
Winds gusting beyond what one could imagine
twisting and turning making a sound
as if a whistle was blowing like a humming bird in distress
setting an alarm alerting that something is quite wrong
not a normal storm water falling at a heavier pace
moving people without a lack of control
water rising high, many people fleeing to a safer place
praying that one will live and not die
I forgot all about the material things
I think about myself and others surviving, life, precious life
there are screams for help to be rescued
trapped, suffering, injuries cuts bruises and some bleeding too
homes destroyed other physical devastation
seeing the dead upon my eyes, what a site to see,
the gruesome smell what a catastrophe
a tragedy that changes peoples way of living
no clean clothes or food to eat, total misery
crying wondering why but when thoughts
reflect on what was once learned about what was written
centuries ago pre-warning us of floods in the holy books
we have seen devastation in foreign lands

Society

now we have a sense of understanding
where they stand now
living without the many necessities
we are living their realities
oh life, how much do we appreciate
heroes regular people like me
lending a hand
helping to donate goods
and rescue those in need.
what a treasury
we won't forget those who died
we mourn their lives
you won't be forgotten
lay a body to rest
a flower will bud again

Conversations: Short Stories

Conversations: Short Stories

Dead But Still Living

There are relatives who have been a part of our lives throughout the duration of our lives and although they are now deceased, they have left some memorable moments upon us.

Both of my grandmothers knew how to get their grandchildren quiet without talking. They used sign language and both of them could get us quiet immediately. For instance, Grandmom Sadie would put her hand up in a stop position and then shake it a few times. We knew right away to be quiet. Grandmom Jesuda would give you a look that had the words all over it "I dare you."

Grandmom Sadie always sat with me around the kitchen table and would have me read the daily bread (a passage from the Bible). Then I had to explain what I read and she would give me her interpretation of what she read. She would always give me scriptures and would always instill a character of kindness.

Grandmom Sadie was an Eastern Star and would take me with her when she was selling her teas for their fundraisers during her visits with neighbors. It was at these times that I saw various interactions with people and business transactions being made; I learned a lot from those ventures.

Realities of Life

Grandpop would fall asleep in his chair and some of us (grand children) would climb up onto his lap. We would take his Chicklets chewing gum out of his pocket. When he awakened, he would say, "Who got me this time?" Grandpop was never upset. He always had another stash of Chicklets somewhere. I did not remember a whole lot about Granddad because he died when I was a little girl.

Grandmom Jesuda instilled a spirit of the fruit with scriptures from the Bible, which inspired me to be positive at such an early age. I often found myself in church watching her direct the choir as a little girl. Grandmom Jesuda would also regularly take me to the store to buy jacks and other small items to play with when I visited her house.

Great Great Aunt Nee Nee lived to be a hundred and three years old. When talking to her on the phone before she would hang up, she would always say, "Alrighty o bye-bye." If you would tell her something good, she would always say, "Oh, I declare." Aunt Nee Nee was very spiritual too. She always would give a scripture for me to read.

Uncle Grice left us his favorite remarks. As children, we would see the ice cream truck and would ask Uncle Grice for some change to buy ice cream. Uncle Grice did not like carrying a lot of change in his pocket

Conversations: Short Stories

so he would ask us, "How much is the ice cream?" We would inform him how much the ice cream cost. Uncle Grice would go into his pocket and pull out some change and begin counting it, and he would say, "I don't have enough money for everybody to get one." All of his nieces would say, "Oh Uncle Grice" and he would respond by saying, "Uncle, my foot!" My sisters, cousins and I would come up with a suggestion of how we could purchase ice cream sandwiches. We told him that we could break them in half and there would be enough for everybody. Uncle Grice would respond with "Gee wiz Christmas!" Uncle Grice purchased the ice cream sandwiches for us and we were happy and grateful.

Uncle Woody would give us money during holiday time and he would always tell us to spend some of it, but make certain to save some too. We saved some coins in our piggy bank. Uncle Woody had a special kind of laugh that was infectious. He would tell a joke and have all of his nieces laughing.

Aunt Ree (Aurelia) would say to me, "Don't let the person that you love outgrow you." That still registers today. Aunt Ree always inspired me to keep pushing on with whatever I wanted to do.

Uncle Leroy loved Aretha Franklin's song "Ain't No Way". He sang it all the time. I truly believe that if a

Realities of Life

promoter would have come through, he would have gotten a contract.

Cousin Mark always had a cheerful smile and would always follow behind his brothers playing tricks on his cousins. Mark could play Scrabble well too. He could beat everybody who played him.

Cousin Avery always had a bubbling personality and always enjoyed having company. She always was full of laughter.

Cousin Darrel always was cheerful too. He always wanted family to get together and enjoy the fun that we used to have back in the days of our youth.

Aunt Elaine could cook fried chicken well and was always sharing her Delta call and stories of her college days with me. She always would include her friend and Soror, U.S. Congresswomen Barbara Jordan, and others in her talks with me. When these Delta sisters were visiting, they always inspired me with using the proper etiquette and intellect while encouraging me to stay focused on positive things.

Conversations: Short Stories

Kitchen Spy

I was just a little girl, at the age of eleven years old, wanting to see what Mommie was up to in the kitchen. When peeking in the kitchen from time to time, I would see her doing various things: placing dishes into the dishwasher, wiping off the counter, and preparing other meals for breakfast. I remember on certain weekends, Mommie would talk to her friend, Helen Greene, on the telephone. She had moved away from Philadelphia to the Philippines because of her husband's employment there. Sometimes I would innocently hear some of Mommie's conversations that involved our family. I would ask Mommie questions about her phone conversation and she would say, "It pertains to grown folks' conversation." She let me know quickly that I was to remain in a child's place, which was not a part of the adult equation. You see, Mommie did not want me to grow up too quickly. She wanted me to enjoy being a child.

After leaving the kitchen, I ran to the living room area to play games with my sisters. Periodically, I would go back into the kitchen to check on what Mommie was doing. This particular time, she was in the kitchen sifting her flour and then placing it in a bowl, adding some water, and using her hands to mix the dough. After mixing the

Realities of Life

dough, Mommie was able to get the consistency needed. Then she would take it out of the bowl and take the rolling pin out (it was a long round wooden rolling pin with big wooden handles) and a cutting board. Mommie would lay the dough out on the cutting board. She would use her hands to shape the dough until it was thick and had the consistency of a good mix. Mommie would roll that rolling pin back and forth like she was playing a shuffle board game; moving slowly and then picking up speed, back and forth until she had it to her liking. Mommie would take out a drinking glass and use it by placing the mouth of the open glass down until it cut into the dough, making a round thick biscuit. Mommie would let me butter up the pan so the biscuits would not stick. After buttering the pan, I would place the biscuits onto the pan. Mommie would place the biscuits in the oven. After awhile, the aroma from the biscuits baking made me hungry. The smell was a good scent that had my nostrils spread wide open and I could not wait for the biscuits to make their delivery from the oven to the table.

  I wanted Mommie not to put the biscuits on the table until the rest of the family was seated so the biscuits would still be hot. Daddy called everyone to the table to eat and I was the first one to arrive and sit down at the table. I was very hungry. I picked up the bread and dropped it immediately. The bread was so hot that it burned

Conversations: Short Stories

a few of my finger tips, which turned red. Mommie said, in a quiet voice, "Put that bread down. We have not blessed the table." So I volunteered to bless the table so that we could eat our breakfast as soon as possible. I was very hungry. I did not like cold biscuits and they did not taste the same reheated to me. We did not have the convenieces of a microwave then. There were none during this time.

    A variety of Grandmom's homemade preservatives were on the table: strawberry, grape, raspberry, just to name a few. I used as many of the preservatives as I could on my biscuits because they all were good. The biscuits were filling to the stomach of someone who was very hungry. Grandmom had it going on! She knew how to make some good stuff. I was so focused on the biscuits that I did not pay attention to the other foods that Mommie had cooked, which was an appetizing breakfast of chicken sausage, eggs, grits, fried potatoes, bacon, apple sauce, chipped beef, fruit, coffee and orange juice.

    On the table by our plates sat a chewable vitamin. Oh, I did not like them and neither did my sisters. The vitamins were so nasty that our dog became our instant disposal for our vitamins. We fed the dog vitamins from underneath the table and he loved them without our parents' knowledge. My sisters and I waited until we were grown to tell our Mommie and Daddy that we fed our

Realities of Life

vitamins to the dog. Our parents both replied together, "What!" They were in total shock. Mommie and Daddy said that they did not have a clue and asked us if we knew that those vitamins were very expensive. We replied, "No!" We were kids then. The thought of how much vitamins cost was the furthest thing from our minds.

Daddy worked two jobs. He was a special education teacher and worked part-time for a catering service. My mother did not work at the time. However, she was a full time homemaker. Daddy said, "No wonder that dog was so healthy." We all laughed and continued eating and telling some great stories with an appreciation of what life brings. Daddy said, "When I have grandchildren, I'm gonna make sure that they take a vitamin that they like." Daddy made fresh Maxwell House coffee in an electric coffee pot. We knew the coffee was ready when we heard it making a perking sound. We ate until we were full and could not eat anymore.

By constantly spying on Mommie in the kitchen, she knew that I had an interest in what she was creating. So she purchased me a small rolling pin from Tupperware and I was well on my way to making some of my own biscuits with Mommie's help.

Conversations: Short Stories

Reunited Again

Isn't it amazing how at some point in our lives we all take time to visit our relatives, usually at funerals? Otherwise we are so consumed with our own nuclear families, work, church, weddings, and other activities that either we don't see or spend very little time with relatives. In another era, life was simple. There were no outside distractions. We never know which road will take us where we want to go; it's not until we meet up again, unexpectedly, that makes it all so special. It is quite interesting how this particular meeting occurred. As a member of a writing organization, we have various activities throughout the year. This year the authors of the Guild displayed their works at one of the area malls. The founder of the Guild, Louis Diggs, has written many books from extensive research on various families in the Baltimore County area of Maryland.

I decided to take a walk around the display areas to look at the various authors' works. I stopped at our founder's table and picked up many books. The founder of the Guild walked over and introduced me to his wife, Shirley Diggs. As we were talking, I was glancing through one of Louis Diggs' books. I became very excited when I saw my maiden name "Muir." in one of them. Shirley said, "I'm a Muir also." We both said, in sync, that maybe we

Realities of Life

---

were related. We began talking about family members and how during the summer time, I would spend a week with relatives on the Eastern Shore. I spoke about my grandmother growing up in Princess Anne, MD and my great grandfather who grew up in Chase, MD. I remember meeting the Cheatam family whom were also a part of the extended family. We had family members from all over the state of Maryland and a few living in the city of Baltimore. I spoke of my father driving the family down from Philadelphia to Maryland to attend a family reunion. When I attended the reunion, I was just a little girl but I remember our family consisted of black and white people. The reunion was a memorable one. There were all kinds of food like you wouldn't believe: seafood, ribs, chicken, pasta, salads and veggies. There were games for the children to keep us occupied and to have us interact with one another. There was music of every kind with people dancing and having a good time. There was much conversation about the family ancestry of yesterday and conversations of goals, which that one day may unfold.

    I remember a woman running out of the room crying hysterically. When I looked at some of the people's faces, some looked surprised while others were laughing and wiping tears from their eyes. I was confused. I had no idea what happened but found out later when I heard a woman ask my mom what prompted the lady to run out of the room. My mom explained that there was a fishing

Conversations: Short Stories

game for the children to play with and the objective of the game was to pick a number and retrieve the fish that had that number. In order to retrieve the fish, you had to be able to hook the fish onto the rod and then you would receive a prize. Well, cousin Mark extended his string on his fishing rod. In doing so, when he swung his fishing rod, his fishing hook attached to a woman's hair. The woman was wearing a wig, and of course the wig came off. Boy, was she embarrassed! To this day, I still hear family members talk about this incident.

Shirley and I revisited finding out if we were related by doing our homework. She would find out by checking out the documentation that had already been researched. So I wrote my dad's name on a piece of paper, along with his sister's and brother's names. Shirley assured me that she was just as excited as I was about finding out if we came from the same blood line. Two weeks had passed and I received a call from Shirley. She let me know that we were definitely related. The two of us were acting like two young school children. We were so excited! Shirley and I spoke of planning when we were going to get together, visit a restaurant and eat. Well, that did not happen. It seemed like every time we were suppose to meet, something would come up and we would have to postpone our meeting. Finally, Shirley telephoned me and we set up a date that would meet everyone's schedule.

Realities of Life

So a date was set and Shirley invited me and some of our cousins over to her home.

When I entered the Diggs home, I was greeted so warmly by all present and was introduced to everyone personally. We sat in the living room area and talked about our ancestry and the good old days that we all participated in at one point and time. We laughed at some of the stories that were told so seriously but funny. We moved our conversations from the living room to the kitchen where Shirley and Louis cooked us a delicious meal. We had ribs, candied yams, potatoes, collard greens, string beans, macaroni and cheese, chicken and dessert. The family sat around the table and conversed about the war and many other issues of today. I was presented with a book that was published called "The Muir Clan From the House Of White". In this book, my family roots go back eight generations. My father's name was included in this book along with my grandmother, grandfather, great grandfather uncles, aunts and other relatives.

The family discussed with me how grateful we were to our relative Sammy Lee Thomas Jr., born in 1961 and a Howard University graduate of 1984. He was one of the founders of the Oriole Historical Society and he researched many of the family members whose names appear in the book. The St. James Methodist Episcopal Church in Oriole, MD (Somerset County) is one of the

Conversations: Short Stories

---

oldest African American churches built by former slaves. In 1885, it was closed and by 1970, it needed to be fully restored. Sammie, along with others, worked within the community to restore the church. I spoke of how I looked forward to meeting and speaking to this extraordinary relative. It saddened me to learn from my relatives that Sammie Lee went on to a higher calling and received his wings to join the good Lord in 1992. He died of respiratory failure at Howard University Hospital located in Washington, D.C.

    I also learned that another relative, Leah (Mary) Sheldon, who was the first person of color to settle in Oriole, around 1815, at the age of 21. During this period of time, Somerset was called St. Peters. It was located on 400 acres. Leah did extremely well during this period of being a free slave. She chose to take in sewing and offered to clean houses of others who lived within her community. With her earnings, she purchased many acres of land and although she and other slaves were free, many of them were recaptured and put back into slavery. There were other stories told of how some of our family members were skilled craftsman carpenters, and built their farm houses and skip jacks (homes). Some relatives farmed their own land and marketed their produce. We are looking forward to adding to this book with other family members and their accomplishments. We are grateful to our family members Gertrude Muir-Steele, Mary Hughes Hines of

Realities of Life

---

the George Muir family, Louis Diggs and Shirley Washington Diggs of Mary Jane Washington's family, who conducted the research for this book. I have had the pleasure to meet them and sit down and carry conversations concerning family.

This book told the history of my family in Maryland and of our Scotland origin. Included in this book are: citations from the mayor (Kurt Schmoke) of Baltimore, a Proclamation designating September 26, 1992 as "Muir Family Reunion Day" in Baltimore, other citations from the president of the City Council, State Delegate and the Governor.

I find that it is amazing how we reconnected. God's purpose for this special meeting was for this particular time. There is a purpose that He has set for us; to cherish every precious moment because tomorrow is not promised. There is a time and a purpose for everything as shown/indicated in the Bible. As we spoke, we talked about how demanding life used to be and how we drifted apart because of family and work responsibilities. Now that we are all older, with less responsibilities of family, it is easier to visit with each other. We vowed to one another that we would keep a connection and stay in touch. We are truly carrying this out by staying in touch by telephone, visitations, and enjoying each other's company.

Conversations: Short Stories

The Family Gatherings Growing Up

My sisters and I would gather together during the Christmas holiday and just enjoy each other's company. We had time off from school and it was something about the holidays that put my sisters and me in a festive mood. We talked about everything: how middle school was a big transition coming from elementary school, for two of us, and how we were learning to become independent by changing classrooms in opposition to staying in one classroom in elementary school. We learned to follow a schedule for classes amongst other things. My younger sister would tell us about the various activities that were happening in her elementary school.

There were special snacks that were available to us during the holiday. Walnuts and Chestnuts were placed on the dining room table and chitterlings on the kitchen table, which we would have once a year. My sisters and I would sit for at least an hour and crack the nuts open and pick out the nuts and eat them. Picking nuts from the shell were hard because they would get caught up in between the grooves of the shell so we used a nut picker to help make the job easier. When we finished eating the nuts, we would discard the shells and clean up the mess we made. We ate so many of those nuts that our mouths became excessively dry and much 'H2O' was needed. After cleaning up, we would have a multitude of things

Realities of Life

going on at one time. The TV broadcasted the Christmas parade while the stereo played holiday and spiritual music.

Mommie and Daddy did not want us to eat much pork so we would only have it during holiday time. Mommie would spend plenty of time cleaning the chitterlings before cooking them. After all, the chitterlings are the intestines of the pig. Mommie would cook the chitterlings in a pressure cooker with vinegar and some of her special seasonings. When the chitterlings were ready, I would eat them hot out of the pot placing hot sauce on top of them. Umm...those chitterlings tasted oh so good!

During this time of the year, we did not mind singing some songs that were old and recorded before our time. For example, Nat King Cole's voice was so mellow and so clear that we would sing "The Christmas Song." This was truly a time that my sisters and I enjoyed. We would sing and while looking into the floor-size mirror on the living room wall, we would dance and choreograph our moves and sing Sister Sledge's song "We Are Family." After we were too tired to continue to dance, we would sit and look at the festivities of the lights that were decorated inside and outside of the house.

Phone calls began to come in from friends expressing to us what they received for Christmas and wanting to know what my sisters and I received as gifts. When I explained that I had not opened any gifts yet, I

Conversations: Short Stories

had to indicate my family's gift opening tradition. That is, no one in our family could open up a gift unless all of us had come together. I would hang up the phone and tell my friends that I would talk to them later. I just wanted to enjoy the rest of my time being home with my sisters!

There were beautiful stockings that were hung from the fireplace that Mommie decorated. The tree that Daddy bought was a big one. If I had to grade my daddy on his tree selection, I would give him an "A". He did an excellent job selecting the tree. I knew Daddy looked at many trees until he could find the right one. When the family would decorate the tree and place a number of lights and ornaments on it, it was even more beautiful. A dove of peace sat on top of the tree along with a handmade angel. Everyone who visited our house throughout the week complemented on how beautiful the Christmas tree looked. When looking at the stockings, one could tell that Mommie was very creative because of the details that she put on each stocking.

After a long morning, it was time for Mommie and Daddy to wake up. My sisters and I had used our time wisely having fun. We anxiously awaited for our parents' arrival downstairs. Our tradition was not to open up presents until family members were present.

Oh, no! How could we forget Aunt Nee Nee? We never had Christmas without her. She was our great aunt

Realities of Life

and a spiritual inspiration to us. Nee Nee was a piano teacher, played often for her church and taught me how to play the piano when I was five years old. She held her piano recitals at Reverend Leon H. Sullivan's church in Philadelphia, PA. The door bell rang and it was Aunt Nee Nee. I opened the door and greeted her with a hello, hug and a kiss.

All of my family approached Nee Nee and gave their hellos, hugs and kisses. One of Nee Nee's sayings was "I declare" when everything was all good. We all sat around in the living room and held various conversations to no end. We all opened our presents and expressed how much we liked all of our gifts. After opening gifts we would place them back underneath the tree. Although we had many gifts, the best gift was the love and affection given by friends and family members who would stop by to say hello and of course stay for some conversation and eat some of the delicious food that Mommie had prepared. We enjoyed their company.

We would often visit Aunt Ernie and Uncle Grice at their home. They lived right around the corner from my family. They were always entertaining guests along with Uncle Timmy. My Uncle Grice loved to cook. There were foods that we as children did not like but when Uncle Grice cooked it, he gave it a different flavor. Aunt Ernie was always talking to us about keeping ourselves up (looking good). She was a beautician and owned her own

Conversations: Short Stories

beauty salon. My sisters and I often visited the salon.

When sitting in the chair getting my hair done, there were many topics, to which I was exposed to. I listened to other customers engaged in conversations, always diversified about race relations, love, society and many others.

My aunt and uncle would shower my sisters, nieces and nephews with many gifts and we were grateful. My aunt and uncle had no children of their own so their nieces and nephews became their children.

My 16th birthday party was held in the club basement of Aunt Ernie and Uncle Grice's house and it still is a memorable one for me. I was allowed to invite up to thirty people to the party and it was hard to choose who would come. I was popular during high school and I knew later on that I would hear some flack about someone who did not get invited to the party. Most of my guests were sisters, cousins, a few friends from the neighborhood and just a few from school. There were all kinds of food and a big birthday cake with my name on it and 16 candles. Everyone sang happy birthday to me and I blew out the candles.

Every record that I liked was sitting right by the stereo console so it was announced by me that it was party time. I was a shy person at times but since I had close family and friends at the party, I was not shy. I used

Realities of Life

Don Cornelius' line from the popular TV show, "Soul Train" and said, "Let's get the party moving!" and everyone stepped onto the floor and began dancing. I loved to party. We danced until we were tired and could not dance any more. I wanted this to be the best birthday party ever. Those of us who sat down to take a rest from dancing enjoyed the conversation of each other. When it was 11 pm, it was time for the party to end. I received hugs and handshakes and some kisses from everyone leaving and telling me that they had wonderful time.

Back to the Christmas holiday, our next stop would be to Grandmom Sadie's house. We would drop off her gift and keep her company for awhile. My aunt was often there when we arrived; she lived at grandmom's house. Other family members would stop by one at a time: Aunt Ernie, Uncle Grice, Aunt Phyllis, Uncle Donald, Merle, my father and mother, Lauren and lil Merle (sisters), Uncle Arthur, Aunt Margie, Aunt Delores, Uncle Warren, Aunt Glorious, Uncle Clint, Aunt Aurelia, Uncle Adolph, Aunt Doris, Uncle Woody and all of their friends. Some of my cousins would be there too: June, Margo, Larie, Tayna, Peaches, Karla, Mark, Aaron, Gregory, Terry and others.

At her house, Grandmom Sadie would talk with her best friend on the telephone, who lived behind her house. If the children were making too much noise, grandmom knew how to work her sign language. She

Conversations: Short Stories

would hold up one of her hands and shake it, meaning that we were making too much noise and if she said, "Children" more than once, we knew that we needed to quiet down. Our cousins of course would be there too. Grandmom enjoyed us and always cooked her specialty meal, chicken and dumplings. We would sit and talk with grandmom about school, church, and camp.

My other family members, lived a distance away so we would see Aunt Dot and Uncle Sesera throughout the year in Orange, NJ. We always communicated with each other by telephone over the holidays. My cousin Vanisha and her husband had a family reunion at their home in Bethlehem, PA. This family reunion was a memorable one. Everyone greeted each other with a hug and kiss. We shared how happy we were to see one another. There were group pictures that were taken and individual ones as well. My cousin had a very large backyard. There was an in-ground swimming pool. Some of us plunged into it and had a good time playing volleyball in the water. There were plenty of other games to keep the children occupied like basketball on my cousin's court and tug of war. There was a lot of fun we all engaged in while playing these games. Others would just sit down underneath the tent, talking and learning a little bit more about what was going on in each other's lives. There were several microphones set up. One of us would step up to the tent microphone and tell how awesome it was coming together, what occupied our lives and what the day meant

Realities of Life

to us. There were some of us who sang, and I enjoyed singing. We had a few comedians in the family. Some of the jokes they told were so funny to me, that I often cried out of joy and laughed for quite some time. After the entertainment, my cousin and I said the blessing, and we began digging into a variety of foods and I believe just about everyone there tried to sample everything. After eating, there was a little more time to converse with family members: cousins Lisa, Shelia, Norman, Norma, Bubba, Cassandra, Darryl, and some few friends who were like family. We said our good byes and hoped to see each other real soon.

One afternoon, my Aunt Phil and her first husband Uncle Donald (Duck) stopped by for a visit, but no one knew the treat that they would receive from me and my cousins. We put on a show of dancing and singing. We were innovative too. We unscrewed the lamp shade and used the lamp as a spot light for the group. We used moroccos as our microphones. Well, I had never seen Uncle Duck laugh so hard before in my life. I sang an Otis Redding's song (a request from my mother). She knew how I could change my voice and go deep. I began singing "Sitting on the Dock of the Bay" and sounded a lot like Otis Redding. I could impersonate Otis Redding well. Everyone began laughing. My Uncle Duck was a fair looking black man, but when he laughed he turned red. His wife said that she had not seen him laugh so hard in

Conversations: Short Stories

years. My sisters and my cousin Karla had the cutest moves and we sounded pretty good too. Just when we started singing one of the Supremes' songs, a fire alarm interrupted our singing. Our cousin Greg said, "I hope those two brothers of mine were not getting into trouble." They were missing from us for a short period of time. Everyone moved quickly to the couch and my sisters and cousin stopped singing. Someone said, "Where was Aaron and Mark?" Aaron and Mark were called and they both responded to the call. My cousins were questioned by their parents and both boys admitted to pulling the fire alarm. The fireman was already in route to our house when we called to explain that the fire alarm was pulled by accident. There were no child abuse laws in place at this particular time so my aunt gave both of my cousins a spanking and spoke with them about the importance of doing what they were asked to do. My aunt informed us, including our cousins, that when they arrived to our house, they were not to touch anything without asking. My cousins Aaron and Mark ended our afternoon of fun and everyone went home.

My mind began wondering. These same two cousins got my sisters and my cousin in trouble once before. We woke up and saw snow on the ground and we wanted to touch the snow. We went outside with our pajamas on right outside of the front door. Aaron and Mark locked us out of the house and we could not get back in. We watched

Realities of Life

our cousins staring at us from the window laughing. We saw nothing funny. We could hear them from the other side of the window saying, "Oooh! You're going to get in trouble!" We were getting cold and they still would not let us in. We were wondering where their older brother, Greg, was in this time of need. Where was he when we needed him? Our cousins left the window and we had no other choice but to ring the door bell.

When my aunt came to the door, we knew we were in trouble. My aunt gave us a lecture about how young ladies do not go outside without the proper attire. Karla heard more arguments than my sister and me from her mother about being outside. Now we look back on this incident and laugh about it.

During the summer, school was out and Daddy would take my sisters and me to Maryland's Eastern Shore to visit our relatives there. My father always spoke of how the family asked him to let his girls spend some time with them. My father thought that it would be nice to get to know some of our relatives. My father agreed to let us stay for a week.

Some of my family ran their own businesses of planting and selling their crops. I enjoyed the family, meeting cousins and playing with them, but one thing I disliked was the outhouses there. I was used to modern conveniences like a nice bathroom inside of the house at home.

Conversations: Short Stories

I would not drink any liquids after 3 pm so that I would not have to go to the outhouse when it was dark. On the Eastern Shore out in the rural area, I was always seeing all kinds of animals running around. I thought that if I went to the bathroom at night, something might grab me. One of my cousins did not make my visits there easy for me. She mentioned sometimes wild animals liked to visit the outhouses at night. My cousin was used to seeing so many animals near and around the outhouse. When it was dark, she carried a flash light. She had no fear seeing all kinds of animals because it was a normal occurence for her.

Relatives on the Eastern Shore invited my family back, but Daddy knew that we only wanted to stay for a day. Daddy tried to convince me to stay for a week. I told him, "I did not want to go back because of the outhouse." It was nearly a year since our last visit and upon entering the house, we received a big surprise while visiting the Eastern Shore. I was asked to cover my eyes with my hands. I was taken by the hand and walked into another room. My relatives told me to take my hands away from my eyes. I took my hands off of my eyes and I saw a brand new bathroom at the residence and it was simply beautiful. I said, "I can go to the bathroom at anytime now." Everyone laughed at my comment.

There were so many other family gatherings that have taken place over the years and have been memorable for me. I believe that, as families, we must continue

Realities of Life

to provide our young children with love and the proper guidance in which way they shall walk, talk and lead others to positive, productive lives.

Conversations: Short Stories

Yesterday's Beginnings

The other day I saw my friend, Althea. We spotted each other from a distance. We were shopping at a large food market in downtown Philadelphia. Althea looked good. Her skin glowed like a shining apple and she was wearing a big smile. The winter cold weather was below ten degrees but it didn't affect Althea. I managed to smile back when we greeted each other. Althea said, "Cheryl, you look great" and I gave the same complement back to her. We were so happy to see each other. We hugged for a good minute and exchanged kisses on the cheek. It was a good meeting. We had not seen each other in a year. We were very close when we were in junior high and in high school, we were inseparable. But when we went off to college, our lives became very busy and we did not see each other as often as we would have liked to. Our priority was staying focused on the academics. However, we did enjoy ourselves socially for a while. During our meeting, we decided that we were going to keep a better job of staying in contact with one another.

Althea asked me how long did I intend to shop. I said probably another two or three hours. Althea said, "Well, I've got some time on my hands for a few hours so why don't we go to Patti Labelle's restaurant and get a bite to eat and talk like old times?" I said, "Sure I'd like

Realities of Life

that." I had never eaten at her restaurant but I have heard from some of my friends that the food and the service were excellent. We brought a few more items from the Farmer's Market and we were on our way to the restaurant. However, we passed some street vendors and stopped to look at some of the items on their tables. I stated to Althea that I always liked most of the things that vendors sold simply because they had some unique items and the prices were usually reasonable. After stopping at one vendor's table, I saw a scarf that I knew my mother would like so I bought it. The price was just right, under ten dollars with taxes included.

    We walked a few more blocks and there was the vendor with a Philly big pretzel. I had to have one of those pretzels. They were always good. Both of us bought a salted, warm, thick, soft pretzel. We did not need the salt but, how often did we get to eat a heated, salted pretzel that tasted so good? It had been years since I had one. I was hungry so the snack would hold me over until I had lunch. Althea said, "Let's get a taxi so that we can sit back and relax." I put my arm up and hailed a cab. As soon as we sat in the cab, the cab driver asked "Where to?" I said, "To Patti Labelle's restaurant." There was no need to give him the address. He said immediately, "I know where it is located." Obviously the restaurant must have been a popular drop off point for the cab driver. Althea said, "I miss the city but I love living in suburbia -

Conversations: Short Stories

Wallingford, PA, right outside of the city." Living in Wallingford, PA was one of the reasons that Althea and I did not see each other often. There was a lot of distance between our homes. I enjoyed the city life and had moved to downtown Philadelphia. I loved living downtown and was close to everything. The only thing that I did not like was my expensive mortgage but I enjoyed meeting with friends and family. I was always going to a broadway play or to hear some of the best singing at the Academy Of Music, or watching a Philadelphia 76ers' game or Philadelphia Eagles' game.

Althea asked me if I saw any of our classmates who lived close to me in the city. I bumped into people all of the time. I saw Beverly and Charla, who were visiting from out of town. Beverly is married and is living with her husband and son in Atlanta, Georgia. Her husband is an officer in the Army and she is running her own computer business and is quite a successful business woman. Pat divorced shortly after she married and ended up moving to Orlando, FL and is successfully traveling all over the world with the airliner, for whom she is working. She is dating an older man whom she says treats her like a lady and wants her to give her hand to him. Girl! Pat needs more time. She wants to make sure that he is the right catch. She has him under very close observation just as if she was studying an insect (scientific experiment) underneath a microscope. She wants to know everything about

Realities of Life

him. Whenever the company sends Pat to Philadelphia, she gives me a call and we go to Chinatown and have a bite to eat and catch up on old times. After all of these years, she never wanted to marry again but she met the man of her dreams and he was older than she was. Pat said the man was a prince and she adores him. It was hard for her not to fall in love with him. He truly knew how to please a woman: he opened doors and let her walk in first, when entering a car, he opens the door and helps her with her coat. He takes her on a vacation every year for a week and while vacationing, he makes sure that they tour wherever her little heart desires. He works a part-time job for money, which he blows on vacations, so that they may enjoy the finer things in life. He surprises her with gifts of flowers, not only for her but also her mother.

I telephoned Althea when I arrived in town from Hollywood, CA and let her know that I was staying in the Hilton Hotel, downtown Philly. Althea said that she would be able to pick me up at 2 pm and take me to her house. Well, the 2 pm pick up became 5 pm. Althea had an emergency with her daughter and had to administer medication to her. Her daughter, Cheryl, was 16 years old and was suffering from Sickle Cell Anemia. Althea explained to me that her daughter's illness was beginning to cause her much pain almost every day. Some days the pain was so bad that her daughter would scream for her

Conversations: Short Stories

to take the pain away. Althea said that her daughter's illness had consumed much of her time, taking her to the doctor's appointments, hospital stays and other activities. During her daughter's last visit to the doctor, she was able to get a strong medication to help her with the extraordinary pain. Althea explained to me that when her daughter was not in pain, she wanted her to enjoy some of the finer things in life. So they would travel to New York and visit the Lincoln Center in New York, and purchase box seats to see Darwin Atwater as he directed his Soulful Symphony.

    This young brother was gifted and knew how to direct a full orchestra of talented musicians. I informed some of my other friends about this talented young man that I saw in New York City. Jackie and Charla informed me that they had just heard a radio announcement that Darwin Atwater would be appearing at the Meyerhoff the month of February in Baltimore, MD. Jackie asked me if I could purchase tickets for them. I replied by saying, "Sure. I will stop by the ticket office tomorrow." Darwin Atwater is part of the latest generation of 2004 that will probably be a household name like the great Duke Ellington. After the concert in New York, my daughter and I would go to dinner at the Ritz hotel's restaurant and I'd let her order whatever she wanted.

    When Althea arrived, she received a phone call on her cell phone. It was Bennett. She was so excited to

Realities of Life

hear from him. I could tell by the smiling glow on her face. Althea's husband, Bennett, was fighting in the war over in Iraq and had been over there for quite some time. He was a high ranking officer in the Air Force and one of the best in the business. He knew how to lead others. It saddened Bennett and the rest of his family when he was given his orders to go overseas especially with his daughter being sick. The military's medical benefits really helped with the expenses of doctor visits, hospital stays and medications. Bennett was earning tax free money overseas which was another benefit of having some extra money. Althea put her cell phone on speaker mode so that we both could talk and hear Bennett. Bennett asked how was Cheryl and I doing. I said, "Fine, but so much better when we hear from you, too." Bennett asked if Cheryl was still staying at her friend's house this weekend?" Althea said, "Yes, she will be home tomorrow. She will give you a call tonight. She told me to tell you she loves you and misses you very much."

Althea said to her husband , "Guess who is here with me?" He responded by saying, "Who?" I responded, "Pat; how are you?" He said, "Fine, thank you." Althea always talked with Bennett quite a few times during the week and told him to always be careful. Bennett told us a few of the horror stories how some soldiers witnessed some of their best friends' heads blown off right in front of their eyes, and how emotionally some of the men are, no

Conversations: Short Stories

---

longer within reality. She told her husband to pray that God will carry him through this difficult time. Bennett said that he would heed to her advice. He also said, "If I don't make it back, I want you know that I love everybody there." She told her husband that he was going to make it back okay and that their daughter and she couldn't wait to greet him with open arms. Althea and Pat always ended our calls with Bennett with "We love you" and Bennett always said, "I love both of my precious ones."

I introduced Bennett and Cheryl to each other when we were kids and they began dating for a few years and then married. I have always been close to them for years, and it does not matter how much time goes by without seeing or talking to one another. Our relationship never changes. We said goodbye and told Bennett that our prayers would be with him, and he said likewise and we ended the call.

Althea began catching me up on her life. She was a good communicator and loved to talk. She talked for a good fifteen minutes with me listening to every word. Althea said to me, "I am doing so much talking and I have not listened to anything concerning your life." Before I could say anything, Althea said, "I got peace in my soul. I lost something so great but because God has always lived inside of my heart, I have peace like a river." Just then Althea's phone rang. I knew something was wrong from the look on her face.

Realities of Life

Althea said she had a family emergency. I said I understand. I said, "Is there anything I can do to help you?" Althea began crying and I tried soothing her by hugging her and saying everything will be okay. Althea said, "I can't talk about it right now. Please, I have to get a taxi." We hailed a Yellow Cab and Althea got in. Althea said thanks and that we would talk later. I said, "Be blessed." and we both waved goodbye. Althea rolled down the window and said, "Call me." and I assured her that I would call. I watched the cab until it was no longer in sight.

Author's Biography

Wanda Muir-Oliver was born and raised in Philadelphia, PA. She currently resides in Ellicott City, MD. She is an educator, mental health worker (independent contractor), motivational speaker (children) community facilitator, singer, actress, entrepreneur and writer. Wanda earned her undergraduate studies (Liberal Arts) at Coppin University in three disciplines: Social Work, Psychology and Special Education. Wanda holds a 90 hour certification in Early Child Care for ages 0 - 9. She also holds a certification in Crisis Prevention Intervention. She is currently working towards a graduate certification in Special Education. Another pursuit is to earn a master degree as a licensed psychotherapist.

Pictured below: The author with her mentor Dr. Dorothy I. Height

050713-100-4-60W